AND IF NOT, HE IS STILL GOOD.

A lesson of surrender and trust when prayers go unanswered.

Julie Boger

DEDICATION

First, I dedicate this book to Jesus. Without Him, this journey would not have been possible for our family. He gives hope when everything seems hopeless.

Second, I dedicate this book to my beloved daughter, Laurie Elizabeth. She brought much joy into my life for 46 years. The memories stored in my heart will continue to bring joy until I draw my last breath.

Last, but certainly not least, I dedicate this book to my son-in-law, Ian McKelvy and Erynn Alexis McKelvy and Reid Douglas McKelvy, my first-born granddaughter and third-born grandson. I love each of you, way down deep.

TABLE OF CONTENTS

FOREWORD

After completing Bible college, I went on to get my degree in Social Work in Abilene, Texas. Soon thereafter, I attended a small group at my church and met my new best friend, Laurie. Being so likeminded in our love for Jesus, we hit it off right away and became very close friends. She introduced me to her mother, Julie, and they were my 'home away from home.' They were a gift from the Lord. It was rare to find Christians who actually loved the Lord first and followed Him wholeheartedly.

Julie hosted a church small group in her home, which I attended. During that season, Laurie and I were praying for Godly husbands, and Julie was a big part of lifting that request up to the Lord with us. There were some uncomfortable first dates I endured, only to run to Laurie and Julie's home where we could talk and laugh about what a terrible time I had! We could laugh for hours at the funny things in life, especially in the dating world. Eventually, we saw God's hand at work when he brought wonderful husbands to each of us. Everything Laurie and Julie did, including preparing for Laurie's wedding, was saturated with mention of the Lord, welcoming Him in every part of their lives. Laurie's wedding to Ian was a sacred celebration of God's love, and His faithfulness. After Laurie married and moved to Roswell, I was like a second daughter to Julie and continued to enjoy seeing her on a regular basis until I married and moved away.

Laurie was my closest friend for 20 years. Together, we shared single life, our weddings, moving to other states, having children, prayers and prayer requests, and lots of laughter through the hurdles of life. If I needed Godly advice, Laurie was the one I would call. She didn't pander, gossip, or complain, but her words of advice came from a deep devotion to Jesus and His Word. She had children a few years before I did, so in most situations, she had been-there, done-that. Our core beliefs were so aligned, I treasured anything she could share with me about her journey.

Even though we lived across the country from each other for the last 15 years of our relationship, she was still my closest, most treasured, most likeminded friend, other than my husband. Laurie never wavered in her trust in the Lord, and she was not a complainer, even when she was sick. Through her journey, we had long conversations about what all her physical symptoms could mean. She was perplexed. Thankful. Brave. Tired. She knew her Lord was calling her home.

Julie tells Laurie's story in a very honest, raw, and personal way. This is her family's experience of holding onto Jesus in the most difficult of times, while searching for answers. Throughout the pages of this book, Julie communicates an underlying truth: Jesus is our anchor. He can be fully trusted; we can always rely on His goodness. In the end, there is nothing to fear. When the world is shaking around us, there is everlasting peace in the eye of the storm. We don't have to be afraid of the truth, and we should in fact, pursue it. That includes medically advocating for those we love when they cannot do so themselves.

My best friend has gone on to her eternal reward. She is full of joy; we will see her and laugh with her again. God is making all things new: "While we look not at the things which are seen, but at the things which are not seen; for the things which are seen are temporal, but the things which are not seen are eternal." 2 Corinthians 4:18 (ASV)

Elizabeth Stultz

FOREWORD

How many of us as parents have had to tell our children "No" about something only to then look at their faces and see their disappointment? Without them speaking a word, we could tell that they didn't understand why we just told them no.

It is never easy when God's plans don't work out the way we think they should. It can be confusing and disheartening when we find ourselves having to submit to the Lord when He answers in ways that don't match the prayers that we prayed.

Corrie Ten Boom, author of The Hiding Place, a story of a family who suffered incredible hardship for hiding Jews during the Holocaust, writes of her own conversation with her father, Casper. "When a train goes through a tunnel and it gets dark, you don't throw away the ticket and jump off. You sit still and trust the engineer."

Laurie and her family have expressed intimately in this book what it is to sit still and trust. Laurie and Julie, her mother, journal beautifully and honestly what it is like to sit still and trust the engineer. In this case, the Father. I so appreciate the way this book expresses the highs and lows, the valleys and mountaintops, hopes and dreams, and even the disappointments. It is a real expression of faith, that even when one doesn't understand, our hope, trust, and confidence is in God. He truly works all things for good, even when we don't see the good in the moment. Laurie's life was a magnificent reflection of bringing glory to God when things don't make sense, and my prayer for you, dear reader, is that you could learn how to do the same.

Randy Turner
Executive Pastor
Beltway Park Church

PREFACE

The loss of a child is a journey that is unimaginable to every parent. It matters not if this child is one or ninety-one! They are still our babies. Any loving parent would willingly take a bullet for any of our children if necessary.

Our family is a family of faith. We never imagined we would experience this unbelievable grief and endure so many ups and downs, highs and lows, deep dark valleys and mountain tops full of hope. I will admit there were times that my faith was tested. That's when lessons were learned, and my praying friends held my arms up. Thank God for prayer warriors.

Who could tell us what to do when no one seemed to know what to do? With each question we asked, we got conflicting answers depending on which physician we talked to. (There were many). This mystery disease baffled even the best of specialists. Our hearts were broken. Laurie was not just another patient in a bed. She was our daughter, wife, mother, sister, aunt, and friend. This didn't seem real to us. I felt as if I was walking under water against the strongest possible current with a pocketful of heavy rocks. The grief was almost unbearable at times.

A dear family friend, Shelley, told Ian and me that after a loved one dies, it takes a year to get your feet under you, and another year to walk without wobbling. That's a great way to express it. There were days I forced myself to get out of bed. . . living life without my daughter was much too difficult.

I have never considered myself a writer. I love a good book but the only thing I've written is a journal and that was for my eyes only. I'm writing this for several reasons. I don't want Laurie's memory to fade. It's important to remember her and talk about her. She talked about writing a book after she was healed to help others going through a valley of uncertainty and darkness. She wanted God to be glorified in everything she did and she lived her life to please Him. I want to write this book to honor Laurie, from a mother's perspective. If this will help one person get through a difficult time it is worth the feelings of inadequacy that I have in writing this.

No matter what happens in our life, God is good. God didn't tell us to understand Him, He told us to trust Him. As a mother, I had to learn some very hard lessons about surrender. God's ways are not our ways. I'm glad we serve a God that we can't understand. If He thought like us, we would all be in trouble.

This is a book about my daughter, but it's also a book about faith, trust, and hope. God did not heal Laurie like we asked. He ultimately healed Laurie when she left this world and stepped into eternity with Jesus, and she received a glorified body with no imperfections.

"Let us not become weary in well doing, for at the proper time we shall reap a harvest if we do not give up." Galatians 6:9

Someday soon I will see Jesus, and I will see Laurie again. That gives me hope and strength to get up every morning. We can never give up! So, we run this race until we win our prize and we do not give up even on our worst day. We look forward to the blessed day we stand before Jesus, face to face.

I've prayed over the pages of this book to be anointed. I pray that it will encourage and bring hope to someone who needs to know that God will never leave us or forsake us. Our prayers are not always answered the way we ask. My hope is that instead of getting angry with God when that happens, you will trust Him. He is a good God.

Julie Boger

"May the God of hope fill you with all joy and peace as you trust in Him, so that you may overflow with hope by the power of the Holy Spirit." Romans 15:13

Chapter 1 HAPPY TEARS - LIFE IS GOOD

Opening the refrigerator, I saw globs of gooey chocolate frosting running down the sides of the tiered cake that I had so carefully decorated the night before. My beautiful cake was mostly bare. The first reaction I had was to scream because the wedding was just hours away. With no time to waste, I hurriedly went into that repair mode that all mothers are equipped with - I call it "the adrenaline overdrive."

I removed traces of icing that remained, made a new recipe and went to work recreating the perfect groom's cake for my soon to be son-in-law, Ian. As I worked on this labor of love, my mind drifted back to how we arrived at this date.

After completing her studies for a Master's degree in counseling and development, my beloved first born daughter, Laurie Elizabeth, had moved back to our home in Abilene, Texas. After deciding she did not want to make her home in the Dallas metroplex, she planned only a short stay, providing time to contemplate her future. We enjoyed a special mother-daughter relationship, so of course, I welcomed her company.

Laurie was my hero. She was special in every way from the time she was a child. I'll always remember the day she was searching the obituary section for Peppe Boger— the poodle mix we adopted from the Dallas SPCA. Our dear pet, Peppe, had darted out the front door and met his demise a few days earlier and our entire family was traumatized. Now, our barely four-year old daughter stood in front of her father and me reading the newspaper to us in great disappointment because the daily news had not mentioned Peppe's name. We had no idea she could read. She taught herself by watching Sesame Street on the television. Astonished, it was difficult to withhold our laughter, which seemed inappropriate for such a serious moment.

I am also reminded of a special Mother's Day that she gifted me with a surprise trip to the Spencer Theater in Ruidoso, New Mexico to see a favorite singing group, Gary Puckett and the Union Gap. This was one of my favorite groups in high school. The weekend was extra special with just the two of us. She grew up listening to all my favorite songs and knew all the words. We made wonderful memories together as we sang, ate, shopped, and laughed all weekend. I will cherish this memory forever.

As Laurie matured, she was beautiful inside and out. She was intelligent, talented, and incredibly funny. She could make me laugh like no other. I admired her strong Christian faith and her dedication to living her life to please God. She had a healthy fear of God and was devoted to him above all else. She desired to meet someone special, someone who loved the Lord like she did. If she didn't find an appealing candidate, she certainly wasn't going to settle for a man who didn't consider God as his top priority in life. She wanted God to choose her mate, so she sat down and wrote out a list of qualities she desired in a husband. It was so detailed, I tried hard not to laugh! She prayed fervently over this list, without wavering in faith. God heard. God answered! Without a doubt, He gave her the desire of her heart.

When Ian entered her life, Laurie knew he was the answer to all her prayers. The checklist of Christian qualities she was seeking in a man were perfectly matched. Ian felt the same immediate attraction to her. They were both looking for someone who was in love with God, and spiritually mature. Without a doubt, God brought them together.

It is rare to see a Christian couple truly follow biblical standards for dating, but they both had strong convictions about honoring God with their relationship. Ian knew and respected that he was dating "a daughter of the King." He took his role seriously. The only challenge to their dating was the 300 miles that separated them. Ian was an attorney in Roswell, New Mexico. They saw each other on weekends and kept the phone lines hot during the week. They sought and followed spiritual guidance throughout their courtship.

An old wives' tale predicts a happy marriage if it rains on your wedding day. The heavens parted and it poured on November 8, 2003, when Laurie became Mrs. Ian Douglas McKelvy.

Their moving ceremony ended with the happy couple taking communion together. The reception was held at "The Grace"—a beautiful building in downtown Abilene, an appropriate reminder of the grace God poured out on their new lives together. Their marriage was a gift from Him, and they knew it.

After they departed for their Colorado honeymoon, I found an eight page letter from Laurie waiting for me at home. A beautifully embroidered handkerchief fell to my lap as I opened the envelope. It was for "catching my tears." My precious daughter knew I would have a good cry that night, but they were happy tears full of joy for my daughter and her new life with Ian.

Ian was made a partner of his law firm on the day of their wedding. I knew this meant Roswell would be where they settled. Together they lived purposeful lives—actively participating in church activities. Ian was occasionally asked to teach at church when their pastor was away. Laurie volunteered as a counselor at Chaves County Pregnancy Resource Center in Roswell. When she saw sonograms of perfectly formed babies in the womb, and heard their tiny little heartbeats, she passionately appealed for the life of the child. Her excitement bubbled over as she shared the reports of young women who, after counseling, chose life for their unborn babies. She was an intercessor and she prayed fervently for these women and babies.

I knew Laurie would be an amazing mother. I had witnessed her compassion and protective nature with her three younger brothers, Christopher, Adam, and Austin—who for a short while—were all in diapers at the same time. She was four when our first son Christopher was born. Adam was born a year later, then Austin followed eleven months later. Their dad was a pediatrician, and we both loved children and planned a large family. I grew up as an only child (apart from some wonderful cousins) till I was seventeen and I did not want that for my family.

Laurie immediately became Mommy's little helper. She kept the boys entertained. One day as she played with them, I heard her repeat a phrase from a popular commercial on television that featured a frazzled woman who dreamed of a bubble bath and escape. Suddenly, my little Laurie said the commercial's tagline, "Calgon, take me away!" We laughed at that memory for years.

Laurie and Ian's first child was born in 2005. A beautiful blue-eyed, auburn-haired baby girl. They named her Erynn Alexis, which means "peacemaker" and "intercessor." She lives up to her name, as she is both. She has an incredibly sweet spirit and a special relationship with Jesus.

Two years later, they were blessed with a beautiful baby boy named Reid Douglas. He had light brown hair, big blue eyes and smiled constantly. He was such a happy addition to the family. The McKelvy home was becoming quite crowded, so they built a new home to accommodate their growing family, including a special classroom for homeschooling. I wasn't surprised when Ian and Laurie decided to homeschool. I used to tease her about being hard-wired to go that extra mile to achieve excellence. She was very detailed oriented and driven to do her best. A supreme organizer, she was either 100% in, or not at all. Erynn and Reid started kindergarten in that room and continue their education there to this day. Trophies, ribbons, and mementos decorate the walls and shelves to remind them of all their accomplishments throughout the years. As they near the end of high school you can see how they have excelled in their studies in that they speak several languages, both are avid musicians, and have authored and published several books.

More than anything, Laurie wanted her babies to know the Lord. She wrote daily prayers and devotions for them. At bedtime, they would pray together as a family, claiming God's promises from Scripture. All those prayers, —for all those years, are organized in multiple three-ring binders for each child—an annual devotion for each year of the children's lives. What a grand trophy for Erynn and Reid. With undaunted determination, Laurie left a legacy of love in those binders. Her love. . . God's love.

When I reminisce about Laurie and Ian together, and reflect on all the wonderful family times, extended family shared on holidays, and visits to their home, I think of all the laughter and happy tears that were shed. I remember the embroidered handkerchief that fell from her eight-page letter she left me on her wedding day for "catching my tears"—my tears of happiness.

How could I know that seventeen years later there would not be a handkerchief large enough to catch my tears of inconsolable grief?

Chapter 2 INTO THE UNKNOWN

On Thanksgiving, 2017, I headed to Roswell to spend one of our family's favorite holidays together. My thoughts reminded me that Laurie had been married 14 years and I wondered how time had passed so quickly. I whispered a prayer of gratitude for my family and how blessed we all were.

As I topped the hill just before Roswell, I chuckled to myself remembering what Laurie had told me on our first trip there together. We were going to her wedding shower and as happy as I was for her, my mother's heart was a little sad that she would be moving to another state 5 hours away.

Just below the crest of the hill, there is a large area of land that is flat and you can see in all directions. On a clear day, the Sierra Blanca mountains surrounding Ruidoso are visible in the distance. As we were driving over the hill, Laurie said to me, "Mom, just look how beautiful this valley is!" I found nothing beautiful about Roswell but she learned to love it there and so I was happy because she was happy. Every time I crest the "hill," I remember how Laurie wanted to convince me to like Roswell.

I was greeted at the door by everyone including their King Charles Cavaliers, Winston and Charles. The house was decorated with fall decor and the scent of cinnamon and spices filled the air. This was Laurie's favorite season, and we talked many hours on the phone every fall, sharing favorite recipes and ideas for Thanksgiving. It was always such a special time for our family, and we looked forward to it all year.

We had an abundance of foods and enough assorted desserts to feed several families. During our meal, I noticed that Laurie didn't eat much. When I mentioned it to her, she said she hadn't been feeling well lately but then changed the subject before I could ask all the "mother" questions. After the table was cleared, we had a fun time of fellowship and laughter playing board games. Our family is very competitive and that always makes it interesting especially during our Scrabble games.

During my visits, I always looked forward to the "alone" time Laurie and I shared after everyone would go to bed. We always enjoyed talking and laughing about silly things no one else would understand. Our mother-daughter bond was special, and tonight was no exception—we had our time alone.

She told me about a few nights before I arrived when she felt bad. She said she just felt like something was going on and she didn't know how to describe it. For the lack of a better word, she said she just felt "weird." She had heart palpitations, chills and felt like she constantly needed to swallow and clear her throat. She felt a "pressure" in her throat, and it concerned her enough that she and Ian went to the Emergency Room in Roswell. The more we talked, the more upset she became and told me that she felt like something wasn't right. She was frustrated because the previous visit to the ER was a waste of time. All lab work and tests were normal, and she was sent home with a diagnosis of acid reflux, leaving doubt in her mind that this was the cause. She told me, "Mom, I think something is wrong with me."

Later that night, the symptoms returned, and I took her to the ER once again because Ian and the kids were in bed. Her blood pressure was elevated which was not normal, for her blood pressure was usually low.

They did a series of vitals, X-rays, lab work, and urinalysis, and after waiting two hours, sent her home once again telling her all tests were normal and for her to follow up with her PCP (primary care physician) the next day. She was relieved that all blood work was normal, but she was unsettled in her spirit that they were missing something. We arrived back at her house after midnight and finally went to bed and got a few hours of sleep. I prayed that God would give someone answers about her treatment and prayed for her to have peace.

The next morning, she seemed better, and our day was uneventful. We had a busy day of activities and more competitive games and crafts.

The time seemed to pass too quickly, and it was time to go back to Abilene on Sunday. I was sad to leave but I had a nursing job to get back to. As we hugged, I assured her I would be praying for answers and if she needed me for anything, I could be there in five hours. The look in her eyes was a little unsettling to me (we mothers pick up on these things). I called my prayer-warrior friends and they agreed to be praying for Laurie's healing. I am so grateful for praying friends! They are such a blessing. The five-hour drive home was a good time for me to talk to God, and I did just that.

This trip to Roswell marked the beginning of our family's journey into the unknown, where we would encounter mystery, heartache, and joy. It began a journey of questions and a desperation for answers that sometimes did not come. We had our faith tested like never before. This was a time of learning how to press in and pray on a level that had never been visited, and quite honestly, I pray daily that we never have to go there again. I've experienced intense spiritual warfare many times in the past, but this was an entirely different level. This was about my daughter—my first-born baby girl.

Chapter 3 HOPE DEFERRED

It would be difficult to record everything that Laurie experienced during the next two to three years following Thanksgiving of 2017. I will tell you that Laurie was on a mission to research everything possible, praying that answers would be revealed. She was sure that something was terribly wrong with her but also convinced that God would heal her. I was praying fervently as well that God would send us "someone smart." As a mother, the hardest thing to go through is to see your child suffer. (I don't care if they are babies or adults—they are still our children). She took it upon herself to ask many questions and sought out experts concerning almost every bodily system. She left no stone unturned. She saw specialist after specialist from head to toe. I doubt if there was any part of her body that wasn't checked.

With each new doctor and each new visit, she would have high expectations of hope in a diagnosis and a plan of treatment, only to be told again and again that everything looked "normal." She was prescribed several medications which did absolutely nothing and was advised to try weird diets that seemed ridiculous. Recent allergy testing revealed she had no allergies. She even had an ER doctor suggest she see a counselor. "Great!" She said, "Now they think I'm looney tunes." With all the diagnostic tests, procedures, lab work, and prescriptions, her symptoms persisted with intensity resulting in her enduring a private misery. She told me once that she could relate to Paul who was afflicted with the thorn in his flesh. Maybe this was her cross to bear, she thought, and at times she felt like God's grace wasn't sufficient as she struggled silently.

After waiting months for a call from the Mayo Clinic, at last she was notified that she was scheduled for an appointment for an evaluation. We were all elated because the Mayo Clinic was supposed to be one of the best health care providers in the US. She had waited so long for this call! She and Ian planned for his mom, Carol, to stay with the kids and they drove over nine hours to Scottsdale, Arizona. They were told to expect a stay of three to five days depending on needed tests. They were prepared to stay as long as needed to finally get answers! Hopes were high and our family was very excited.

After checking into their motel just across the street from the Mayo, and getting a good night's rest, they arrived the next morning for the first consultation. They were impressed with the first doctor as he took extensive notes and spent a long time listening and asking questions. He appeared very compassionate and highly educated. He scheduled her the following day to see other experts and told her she would be having many tests and scans and reassured her that this would continue until they had answers and a diagnosis as well as a plan of treatment.

Laurie called me that evening and I could sense the excitement and hope in her voice. I hadn't sensed this in months, but my heart leapt with joy for her and Ian. Her hopes were high. She commented to me, "Mom, I feel very encouraged about this place—they are professional, and this doctor actually listened to me! He is taking me seriously." We all slept well on this night for the first time in a very long time.

Early the next morning as Laurie was getting ready for her busy day of appointments and tests, the phone rang. The secretary from Mayo was on the line and regretfully informed her that the clinic had indefinitely stopped taking outpatients or doing any diagnostic testing. She continued to explain that due to COVID being rampant in New Mexico, the governor had ordered the state to shut down. No exceptions. She proceeded to tell her to go back home and gave no indication when a follow-up visit would be rescheduled... SERIOUSLY???? We were all in disbelief and speechless. Laurie and Ian had waited months for this day. They had spent a lot of money for this trip and made so many arrangements, not to mention they drove nine hours just to be told to turn around and go back home! This was so wrong! "Hope deferred makes the heart sick." (Proverbs 13:12) We all felt sick.

There were no words to describe the disappointment. As a mother, I couldn't fix things this time. That's what we mothers do... we fix things for our kids. It's in our DNA. My heart was so heavy. I was reminded of Romans 8:28, "And we know that all things work together for good to those who love God, to those who are called according to His purpose." The scripture above this one tells us that the Spirit helps us in our weaknesses—for when we do not know how to pray, the Spirit intercedes for us. I struggled as I prayed for understanding. I had to stop and remind myself that my faith and hope was anchored on God's word and not on my feelings. My foundation is JESUS and when we don't understand, He sees the big picture when we can't. God didn't tell us to "understand Him," He told us to "trust Him." I surely did not understand why this happened and to be honest, I still struggle with it. Someday, I will know.

After arriving back in Roswell, Laurie tried fervently to put depression and disappointment aside by staying focused on God's goodness and by staying busy. She was extremely organized and kept her house immaculate even though she was struggling. She continued to seek out experts and more doctor visits followed. This mystery continued to be unsolved and I continued to pray for "someone smart." My cherished friends continued to intercede for her, and they would call and text me about their prayer times. Some had visions and some had words of encouragement.

My church family, Laurie and Ian's church family, and many friends prayed. The prayers are what kept us going by bringing us much needed strength and hope. It seemed like someone would always call at just the right moment when we needed a scripture. Prayer is a powerful weapon!

On Thursday nights, Laurie and Ian had a date night. They would set aside time just for each other and always looked forward to that. On the other nights, she cooked delicious meals for her family. Between homeschooling, church activities, sports, piano lessons, and competitions, and everyday activities, she did an amazing job. There were days when she called me for prayer and encouragement. As we prayed, tears would flow in Texas and in New Mexico because we both felt so frustrated that this mystery had not been solved yet. She didn't like to complain and tried not to, but there were days that she honestly didn't know if she would make it. She had symptoms that continued and were so random that nothing seemed to make sense. She would sweat at night so much she would have to change her pajamas. She had headaches often and insomnia continuously leaving her tired and emotional. She felt pressure in her neck and had constant drainage causing her throat to be sore. She developed tinnitus and occasionally, she had nausea and felt dizzy. Her heart would palpitate, and she felt anxious, causing more stress on her body. The lack of sleep started to take its toll on her, and she was just very tired.

She would sometimes go to the guest room to sleep because she didn't want to keep Ian up all night. Erynn told me once that some nights she would hear her mother crying and praying and that broke my heart. Some nights she would call or text me and we would pray together until she felt better. She didn't do that often because she didn't want to upset anyone or be a burden and I told her countless times that she could never be a burden to me! Laurie was a woman of strong faith, and she believed that God would heal her in His timing. She knew God loved her but until her healing was manifested, she didn't want to be a complainer. My heart breaks knowing how long she dealt with this.

Again, included in my daily prayers was for God to send us "someone smart"— someone who was a believer and who would hear directly from the Holy Spirit. I asked for revelations from God and for this mystery disease to be identified and destroyed. This was affecting our entire family. God tells us in John 10:10 that Satan comes only to steal, kill, and destroy. I prayed for Satan to get his filthy hands off of God's property and reminded him that she was covered with the blood of Jesus. I knew as a believer that we had authority to turn back darkness and doubt. I asked God to show us how to pray and sat in silence many times not knowing how to pray, so I prayed in the spirit. I was reminded of the words of Jesus in John 10:10, "I came that they may have life, and may have it abundantly." I claimed that my daughter had an abundant life and declared that she was healed in the name of Jesus. We all stood on His promises and when the enemy would come in like a flood, we silenced him with the word of God. I prayed so much there were days that I didn't have strength to say a word but communicated with God through my tears. He understood. It was during those times that my precious friends held up my arms in prayer. I have a deep love for those dear ones that never gave up and continued to lift Laurie up to the throne room of God in prayer and intercession. I will forever be grateful for true friends. They were the perfect example of what the church is supposed to look like.

Chapter 4 "SOMETHING IS NOT RIGHT, MOM!"

Laurie and Ian were determined to live life as normal as possible despite this uninvited mystery disease that had invaded their family. Being careful not to create more stress for Erynn and Reid, they were honest with them about their concerns for their mom. They spent a lot of time together and enjoyed several vacations across the United States. One of their favorites was the Grand Canyon, as they loved the majesty of God's creation displayed in beautiful sunsets and earth tones of copper and crimson in canyons and crevices as far as the eye could see.

In the summer of 2020, they took a road trip to North Carolina to visit Ian's dad, Warren, and stepmom, Roberta (Rob). Making many stops along the way, they sent photos of each state line and a brief description of where they were headed next. They planned to visit the replica of Noah's Ark in Williamstown, Kentucky and they were most excited about that.

I believe God gave them such a sweet gift during this time. Laurie felt well on most days and was able to hike to the mountain top with the family. It would be their last vacation together but full of such wonderful memories and pictures. I have a framed photo of her on a swing with her mouth wide-open with laughter. I will always cherish this because I can just imagine the laughter she is having in Heaven right now, and the joy she is experiencing.

August 11, 2020: I was excited when they drove up in my driveway to spend the night on their way home from vacation. They were all tired, but we had a wonderful evening of food and conversation. We had a good night's sleep and the next morning after breakfast they headed back to Roswell.

Laurie had been coughing a little, but after they got home, she developed a persistent cough and just didn't feel well. Reid had a cough also, so she thought they had just caught a cold. Reid got better, but Laurie got worse. She ended up going to several walk-in clinics during a 2–3-week period because she had developed some shortness of breath which caused concern. As usual, she had various diagnoses and was given prescriptions for antibiotics and antifungal medications along with a nebulizer. Nothing seemed to help, and she was continuing to grow weaker. She was tested several times for COVID, and all were negative.

We texted and talked back and forth, and she kept telling me, "Something is not right, Mom!" I called my prayer warrior friends again and they all agreed to pray for her. I prayed my usual prayer—for God to send us someone smart. I asked God to send her someone who was filled with the Holy Spirit and who could hear the voice of the Lord. I felt so helpless five hours away. She was taking meds and at this point we didn't know what else to do but to trust that the antibiotics and other prescriptions would soon start to strengthen her immune system.

After several weeks of antibiotics, anti-fungal drugs, nebulizers, and office visits, we saw her decline. She was growing weaker, and nothing seemed to help.

October 16-18, 2020: When I arrived at Roswell, Erynn and Reid met me at the door and led me to Laurie's bedroom. Immediately our eyes locked—it was a mother-daughter communication without saying a word. My baby girl was very sick. Her face was flushed, and she was weak. I spent the entire weekend lying beside her praying and trying to comfort her. Silently, I felt guilty for not coming sooner. The physicians she had been seeing for the past month did absolutely nothing to improve her condition. I was needing comfort more than I wanted to admit and was very worried for her. This was not our typical, full of life Laurie. She had an appointment the following Thursday with her PCP and we had insisted that something had to be done to find out what was going on. I was stressed that she had to wait until Thursday, but it made leaving her on Sunday afternoon a little easier. Ian assured me that he would call as soon as her appointment was over, and he would take good care of her. I left with a heaviness in my spirit. I had to work on Monday, or I would have stayed longer.

October 22, 2020: I could hardly wait for my phone to ring. Laurie called me as soon as her appointment was over and said, "Mom, I have double pneumonia...I knew something was wrong!" No wonder she had been so sick. "Oh, my goodness, Laurie," I said, "I'm so sorry! I'm coming to Roswell!" Ian then told me that her doctor did a chest X-ray and a CT scan of her chest and abdomen. The doctor was very concerned with the pictures because they appeared to show that she had nodules in both lungs with an appearance of ground glass.

Obviously, this was not a normal image of the lung tissue. This was very alarming. Her PCP knew of a good Pulmonologist in Carlsbad which was 90 minutes from Roswell. She called and the earliest appointment was October 27th. My mother's heart wanted to SCREAM! Nodules??? What on earth does this mean? Ground glass appearance? October 27th? That's 5 days! NO! She will not be put off for five days! This is my daughter we are talking about. Who are these crazy people to think she will just lie there for five more days and continue to grow weaker? NO! This is so wrong!

I made arrangements to take time off from work and made plans to go to Roswell. No job was more important than my family. God would provide, He always had, and I knew He always would.

Chapter 5 THE DREADED "C" WORD

The local weather forecasted snow for October 27th. Ian decided to be safe and take Laurie to Carlsbad the night of the 26th so there would be no problem with the roads. They checked into the hotel and as they were getting on the elevator, Laurie doubled over in intense pain. She had been coughing so much, she told Ian she felt like she had cracked a rib. She was complaining of her side, back, and shoulder hurting. Alarmed, Ian immediately took her to the Emergency Room at Carlsbad Medical Center and the Pulmonologist met them there. Obviously, she was too ill to transfer anywhere so they admitted her right away. She was administered oxygen, IV fluids for dehydration, antibiotics, and steroids. Multiple vials of blood were drawn. She was a very sick girl. This was during the worst of COVID, but our family will forever be grateful to the doctors for allowing our family to be with Laurie. We had God's favor, and we knew it—one of our many God stories throughout this journey. They made a huge exception knowing how sick she was.

I was driving to Carlsbad when Ian called me. He proceeded to tell me about the incident on the elevator and the pain she had been in and how serious her condition was. I felt as if the highway had melted under my vehicle as I tried to keep it on the road. This wasn't happening. I prayed. Then the line went silent for what seemed like an eternity. Finally, with a cracked voice, Ian said, "There is a possibility that Laurie has cancer."

NO!!!!!!!!!! Immediately when I heard the dreaded "C" word my body refused to breathe. I tried to say something. . .anything. . .but I was frozen. No words would form in my mouth or my brain. My brain was malfunctioning.

Thoughts were bouncing around in my head like popcorn on a hot fire. GOD! Will my baby girl have to endure chemo? Is this treatable? Will she suffer with pain? Will she throw up and lose what little weight she has left? Will she be scared? What about her hair? (It was silly to think about her hair, but my mind was all over the place.) Should I sell my house and move to Roswell? Do I need to quit my job right away? Will she be home for Thanksgiving...for Christmas? What if she doesn't make it, God...are you telling me that Laurie may die? NO!!!! God, I want to remind you that we are talking about my first born. This is my daughter. She loves you with all her being God. I'll take the bullet...please give this to me and let my Laurie live. Let her rise and be healed and walk out of this place. I begged God even though I know we don't have to beg. I've never begged so hard in my entire life.

My sweet girl was 45 years young. She had always been full of energy and healthy apart from occasional colds and the usual seasonal bugs people would get. She exercised regularly and ate healthy. She and I had been known to shop all day and never tire. There is nothing anyone could have said to me at that moment to snap me back to reality. I was in total disbelief and denial. How could I fix this? As mothers, we fix things for our kids—that's what we do. We wash the wound, apply antibiotic ointment, apply a Band-Aid, kiss our kids, and send them out to play.

This needed more than a kiss and a band-aid. We needed a huge miracle, and we believed our God was a God of miracles. We were expecting a miracle. Our churches and friends were believing and praying with us in agreement. The elders at my church at Beltway in Abilene even prayed over and anointed a blanket and sent to her. Randy Turner, the Executive Pastor at my church called or texted almost every day for months and prayed for us. I will forever be grateful for him and for my very special girlfriends whom I love deeply. We got strength from those prayers. Honestly, without them I wonder if we could have kept our sanity.

There were six of us crowded in Laurie's small hospital room for five days. The nurses brought in an extra bed and two more recliners. It was practically elbow-to-elbow. We never left her bedside, except in shifts to go shower and change clothes. I was not comfortable with this small hospital, and less impressed with some of the nurses...we questioned everything they did and every medication they gave her.

Rivers of tears flowed from all of us. Our hearts were breaking and to see Laurie struggling for breaths was torture for us all. She had oxygen as high as eight liters at times, not to mention tubing, alarms going off, and blood being drawn constantly. We became acquainted with a grief we had never known. Of all of us, Laurie was the strongest in the room. She would ask Erynn and Reid to lie beside her as she comforted them with her words. It broke my heart.

She asked for a notebook and a pen because she wanted to write us all letters. I can still see her lying there with the oxygen mask on, fervently writing letters to us, barely able to take a breath without a struggle. She was determined to write them. Her faith was so strong, and she told us she was not afraid to die. She even talked to her doctor about Jesus and how she was sure she would be with Jesus as soon as she drew her last breath. She asked him if he was sure. He was not a believer, but I know he must have thought about what she said to him!

I was unable to read the letter she so carefully wrote to me for a long time. It was just too painful.

There were two main doctors working on Laurie's case. We were constantly waiting on lab work and test results. We discovered that on weekends not much was accomplished in the hospital. We were beyond frustrated and incredibly stressed. We prayed endlessly that she didn't have cancer, that this was just one huge mistake. I was watching my daughter struggle to breathe and there was not one thing I could do about it. There are no words to describe how I felt. My mind was trying to process options for her. How could we get her out of this hospital and transferred to a better equipped hospital? She was so sick.

I wrote this in Laurie's hospital room at Carlsbad when we were given the "death sentence" and told she had cancer with a life expectancy of five days:

"I grieve for my first-born as I watch her lie in this hospital bed as she struggles to take a breath. I just want to breathe for her. I want to let this cancer ravish my body and leave hers. How dare this tormenting disease trespass on God's property. My beautiful Laurie. Daughters are special. They call you when you're lonely. They send cards for no reason. They make sure you have Mother's Day gifts and birthday gifts and call you about recipes. They laugh with you and at you and act goofy when you're trying to be serious. They are perceptive when things aren't quite right. They make Thanksgiving and Christmas and New Year's and birthdays special with their personal touches that only a daughter can do.

I don't think I can do life without my daughter...I know I will—because you, God, will enable me, but it's not going to be doable without you!

I ask why, but I get no voice from heaven with an answer. Why would a wonderful mother who has home schooled since day one, a beautiful wife who adores her husband, and an amazing daughter, sister, and friend be taken away from our lives? I have no earthly idea. Only you know, God. You have the heavenly answer. I can only imagine what you have in store for this amazing daughter of mine.

She's felt bad for three years. I've heard her say many times, "If the Lord doesn't heal me, then I've told Him to take me home. . ." She's tired. She's very tired.

I want to tell her to fight with all my being. I want to tell her to kick Satan in the butt and rise and be healed. I want to tell her I love her until it saturates every cell in her frail body. I don't want her to step out of this realm called earth without knowing how much she is loved by her mother. I don't want her to step out of this realm at all, God.

I feel totally helpless but not totally hopeless. I'm still believing you are the God of miracles, but if she is not healed here, I know you have other plans. God, you see the big picture. This is so hard!

I'm not ready to give her back to you God. Help me Lord, I'm really needing you right now. I watch Ian massage her frail and bruised arms from IV's and needles, and I see her trying to be brave. I know she wants to break down inside and scream at the top of her lungs. She is the strongest and bravest person I have ever known. She is my hero. Jesus, come quickly."

Chapter 6 THE OCTOBER THAT CHANGED EVERYTHING

We were told repeatedly that test results were being processed. We were always waiting on answers, and they were extremely slow in coming. I would watch Laurie struggle to breathe and would catch myself taking deep breaths as if that would transfer over to her. Her face was puffy from steroids and her skinny little legs and ankles looked like they belonged to someone else they were so swollen. On her high school basketball team, they teased her with the nickname "Bird" because her legs were so thin. She complained of pain in her back and shoulders and had a deep raspy cough. Her nose was raw from the high concentrations of oxygen and the nasal cannula was making her mucus membranes raw. They had to switch her over to an oxygen mask because she required more oxygen than the cannula could provide. Due to all the antibiotics, she had developed a mean case of thrush and was made to rinse her mouth with bad tasting medication. Ian was constantly applying non-petroleum gel to her nose and lips. Bless this child of mine, she was so miserable.

We had amazing friends who had meals delivered to us. One day we had so much food, we shared with the nursing staff. When God provides, He doesn't do it half-way. He is a God of abundance. I sat beside Laurie as often as I could. I just needed to touch her—I needed to feel her pulse. Somehow, I felt if I could hold her hand, she would be okay. The oxygen mask restricted Laurie from talking much to us and I would tense up every time she would take it off to say something. I wanted every bit of that precious oxygen to penetrate every cell in her lungs and her blood.

I will say that the atmosphere in the room was very somber at times. When one of us would start crying it was a domino effect. I could barely look at the kids without crying. Then I would watch Ian attending to her and start all over again. Ian's mom, Carol and I went through several boxes of tissue.

Then, after we all had a good cry, someone would say something to make us laugh. It was an emotional roller coaster. On top of everything, we weren't sleeping because the nurses were in every 2-3 hours taking vitals, answering alarms, drawing blood, and giving medications. My recliner was beside Laurie so I could hold her hand and I think one could have stored raw meat in there. It was so cold I was sure I would get pneumonia too.

October 28, 2020: Laurie was scheduled for a lung biopsy that day. We dreaded it for her so much, but she did well and by the mercy of God didn't have any complications except soreness. The local pathology reading was "inconclusive" and was sent to the Cleveland Clinic. The X-rays of her lungs revealed worsening of the nodules and an elevated CA-125 (cancer screen). There was rapid deterioration of the nodules indicated in the images. This is not something we were prepared to hear.

The doctors came into her room with somber faces and told us that she had a very aggressive cancer that they believed originated in her ovaries and metastasized to her lungs, liver, ribs, and possibly her spine. We were then told that she had days to survive. . . five days at the most.

I was in another realm. I was spinning faster than I could comprehend. WAIT JUST A DARN MINUTE!!!! Let's start this conversation over because I need you to repeat what you just said. I'm pretty sure I didn't hear what you just told us. First, let me throw up because I'm pretty sure I'm going to be sick. Everything immediately went into slow motion, and I felt numb. NO GOD! Please NO! This can't be the truth. These doctors are crazy, and they have no clue. They don't know Laurie like I know her—she would never get cancer!

I barely remember the conversation after that as the doctors discussed our options. She could remain at the hospital in Carlsbad until her time was up or we could take her home to be on hospice. They told us there was nothing else they knew they could do for her. What? There is always something that can be done! They were giving up. This was unbelievable!

They just told us we can go home and be comfortable? What a joke! Are you seriously kidding me? Nothing else you can do for her? I don't believe this. Hospice is for the dying patient and Laurie is not going to die! She is just very sick and needs someone smart. What kind of a place is this that gives no hope? Come Lord Jesus and get us out of this place!

Thankfully, Laurie and Ian had much more sense than I did, and they were discussing the options. Of course, Laurie wanted to go home where she felt the most at peace. We would agree to hospice only because we needed oxygen and drugs and equipment. We would do this until we could get her transferred to M.D. Anderson or somewhere. . . anywhere. . .where there was someone smart. When the biopsy result was ready, we would have a correct diagnosis and we could get her admitted where people would give us hope. M.D. Anderson was our goal. Little did we know that God had other plans. He's much smarter than us.

As sick as she was, she told her doctors again that she was not afraid to die. She didn't want to leave the love of her life, Ian, and she didn't want to leave Erynn and Reid or her family. She had peace about whatever God wanted to do. It was well with her soul. If only I could have been strong like her. I was a mess. I believe in the power of our words and know that prayer is powerful. I've seen God do amazing things in people. He is a good God. But I was struggling.

In a strange sort of way, Laurie was almost relieved. She said at last she finally felt validated. For over three years, she had been telling everyone that something was terribly wrong with her and no one took her seriously. She had even been told by an ER physician to consider getting counseling! At last, now people would believe she was not crazy. She had been very sick for a long time. I'm sorry that she suffered for so long but her faith in God never wavered. Oh, God. . . give me faith like my daughter had. What a trophy of grace she was.

Did we cry? Oh, yes! Like never before. It was the saddest day ever. There are no words in the English language to express our pain and grief. How do you comprehend something like this? It was a dark time—a place we had never been before. A place too difficult for us to deal with. This was a job for God because He alone was the one who could help us.

We called our family, and they came to visit Laurie thinking this may be the last time they saw her on this planet. We still had no report from the lung biopsy and no definite diagnosis even though the Carlsbad doctors thought it was cancer. We needed confirmation from the biopsy.

November 2, 2020: She was discharged from Carlsbad. We loaded up oxygen, tubing and medications and headed toward Roswell. She tolerated the ride home without too much discomfort, although she was sore from the biopsy. It was a relief to be leaving the hospital but very unsettling about the journey ahead of us.

Chapter 7 THE AGONY OF WAITING

Hospice came to the house and Laurie was admitted the same day. They supplied the needed oxygen and equipment as well as medications she took round the clock. Ian was so diligent to keep a detailed record of meds and the time the next dosage was due.

We believed Laurie would recover. Hundreds of prayers were going up constantly for her. The difficulty was waiting for reports and test results. We were desperate for a diagnosis from the biopsy so she could be admitted at M.D. Anderson, or somewhere. . . anywhere besides Roswell or Carlsbad! Ian was on the phone frequently making arrangements for a transfer and trying to connect with someone who could help us get her admitted without a diagnosis. We were beyond frustrated especially with the Cleveland Clinic for being so slow with sending the biopsy report. I knew every hour wasted was time she could be receiving treatment. Once again, I had to remind myself that I couldn't fix this. It's so hard to surrender to God sometimes and total surrender was one thing He taught me through this emotional journey. It was such a hard lesson to learn because fixing things for my children is in my DNA.

Laurie was spiking a temperature of 103°. Ian was giving meds as often as she was allowed, and we would put cool packs on her to reduce the fever—this went on for days. She was so weak, Ian carried her to the bathroom because she was unable to walk alone, and she was barely able to eat because she had sores in her mouth and throat making swallowing very painful. She developed a new symptom of chest pain when she swallowed. My mind was racing with accusations from the father of lies that her cancer was spreading. I was determined not to listen to Satan, but to stand on God's word: "By His stripes we are healed." (Isaiah 53:5) It seemed as if there was a war going on in my mind. . . I constantly quoted one of my favorite scriptures found in 2 Corinthians 10:5, "We cast down every high and lofty thing that exalts itself against the knowledge of God and bring every thought into captivity to the obedience of Christ." It's amazing how God's word changes the atmosphere and brings peace to our spirit when we say it out loud.

One of the pieces of equipment that Hospice brought was a hospital bed. She didn't like it, so we moved her back into her bed which was much more comfortable. I was happy because we could all lie beside her now (including her co-dependent dogs) and we could hold hands. The room was fragrant with beautiful flower arrangements our friends had sent and it was peaceful for her except when the fever spiked, and she felt so bad. I didn't want to leave her bedside any more than necessary and appreciated that their church was amazing and brought wonderful meals to our family during this time. She didn't have much of an appetite but when she said something sounded good to her, I would have driven out-of-state to get it! We were happy when she got a little nourishment even if it was only a few bites at a time.

November 8, 2020: What a special day this was for Laurie and Ian—their seventeenth wedding anniversary. She was so sick but determined to get dressed and get out of bed for a while. She and Ian drove around for a short while and had some alone time even if it wasn't their idea of the perfect anniversary date like they had spent every year in the past. She immediately went to bed when they came home, and I know that was hard for her. We were still waiting on reports and every time the phone rang our hearts leapt with hope that it would be news.

November 12, 2020: Finally! The Cleveland Clinic released the long-awaited report. It showed T-Cell infiltrates, possible T-Cell lymphoma. But the sub-type was still unknown and inconclusive. In other words, they still had not determined for sure what this mystery disease was. So, now what? Where do we go from here? Where does one go when no one seems to know where to go? Ian was diligently seeking advice and counsel and we were becoming more and more anxious with each hour. M.D. Anderson wanted a definite diagnosis. It just didn't make sense to us. Nothing made sense.

November 16, 2020: The PET scan showed worsening of the nodules, but they were isolated in her lungs. It was not what we had hoped to hear but we were trying our best to stay positive and trust that God had a plan. She also had a bone marrow biopsy and tolerated the procedure well. I prayed that she would be strong enough to go for those tests because she was so ill. By God's grace she was able.

November 17, 2020: The bone marrow report was normal. Hallelujah! Although we were devastated about the lungs worsening, we had hopes about the bone marrow being normal. We clung to every ounce of positivity we could get. With disappointment came desperation. . . desperation to get her out of Roswell! Our problem was finding someone to admit her. Keep in mind, this was during the worst of COVID, and most hospitals were full. The doctors called everywhere and even Tucson, Arizona was full. We considered Lubbock but there was an issue with insurance out-of-state. Not having a definite diagnosis was a problem too. It seemed as if all the doors were closed, and we spent many hours on our knees interceding for a miracle. It seemed so unfair to watch our precious girl struggle and feel so helpless. We didn't know at the time, but God did not want Laurie to go to M.D. Anderson. He had other plans for her. We just needed to get out of the way and let God be God.

After much prayer and many sleepless nights, Ian felt impressed to get in touch with a friend who conveniently had connections to an Oncologist in the Denver, Colorado area. He was working in the Colorado Blood Cancer Institute, located at Presbyterian St. Luke's Hospital in Denver. Miraculously, we got Laurie scheduled to see him!

November 19, 2020: Ian, Laurie, and I packed up the van and left early this morning for Denver. His mom, Carol, would stay with Erynn and Reid in Roswell and make sure they didn't miss their computer classes for homeschool and take them to piano lessons. We had 16 cylinders of oxygen to take with us because she required so much concentration. We had planned to fly, but the FAA regulations prohibited the use of eight liters of oxygen. We were disappointed about that, but after we arrived and settled in, we understood that it happened for a reason as we would be needing our vehicle during our extended stay.

Ian had to pull over every hour and forty-five minutes to change her oxygen cylinder all the way to Denver. Thank God she slept most of the way and our prayers were answered that she tolerated the trip so well. Even though she felt so ill, she still had a sense of humor and had us laughing when she had to stop once for the ladies' room. Ian and I were on each side of her holding the oxygen tank and maneuvering all the tubing, being careful to keep it off the floor. The last thing we wanted was for her to contract an infection.

Chapter 8 DENVER AT LAST

The Rocky Mountains of Denver never looked so good! We made it in time to check into the Marriott with 30 minutes to spare. That gave us time to freshen up before heading to Laurie's appointment.

When we arrived at the hospital, we were led to an exam room and the first thing they did was test her for COVID. It seemed like we waited forever to finally get to talk to the doctor. She was exhausted and fading fast. She had only taken a few bites of food all day, but I was able to flag a nurse down and she brought her some macaroni and cheese. She was beginning to look flushed with a fever and after eating, complained about how her chest hurt when she swallowed. We got her to drink some juice and we waited and waited for the COVID results. Ian answered hundreds of questions about Laurie's history while we waited. Finally, the COVID test came back negative, confirming four or five previous tests performed in Roswell and Carlsbad.

Ian and I were prepared that we might not be able to stay with her in the hospital because of COVID but we were not ready to let her leave us. We were disappointed that we couldn't go with her to be admitted and not allowed to visit her room at all. The healing process depends a lot on one's state of mind and being alone and isolated is not good. At this point, we were just relieved that she was finally in a hospital that hopefully knew what they were doing. We once again were determined to focus on the positive. We could not change the hospital policy, unfortunately, as they made it clear there were no exceptions. This was cruel to restrict family members from being with loved ones when they are sick. She was in a strange place and aside from feeling awful, she was fearful of what was ahead of her. I just wanted to hold her hand. . . to touch her. From a mother's perspective, we needed to touch! I needed to lock eyes with her, and I needed to be in her room. We would have gladly taken a COVID test to be with her but that wasn't an option. We said our fast goodbyes and I cried all the way to the car. We were at the hospital's mercy. We just left our precious Laurie in the hands of total strangers and were trusting that God would take care of her. He was our rock that we leaned on 24/7. I prayed that He would send us "someone smart." Surely, this place had a lot of smart people!

Ian and I prayed for the hospital, the staff, all the patients, and their families. We drove around the perimeter and asked God to bless them all and to take care of our girl who was so sick. We rebuked all evil and asked the Holy Spirit to fill her room so that everyone who entered would feel the presence of God. We asked God to station ministering and warrior angels in her room and we prayed against any errors that might be made.

This facility was very good to communicate with Ian about her condition, tests, procedures, and opinions. They were also good at listening to questions Ian and I had and answered them all with patience and satisfying answers.

Laurie was assigned a dozen physicians on her case. This was a mystery disease no one knew anything about, and they were dedicated to giving her the best of care and to make a diagnosis. She had a specialized doctor for almost every bodily system. Once, Laurie had a meltdown and as she was crying, she told the doctor she was fearful that they would never make a diagnosis because of the years she had been suffering with this. The doctor assured her they would get to the bottom of this and find out what was wrong with her and that brought her comfort. We were so thankful for FaceTime together! Without that it would have been miserable. When she felt like it, we would all talk to her and most of the time she was begging us to get her out of there! She was not a good patient during this time, and it broke our hearts. She wasn't thinking rationally—all she knew was that she wanted to go home. She had not been away from Ian and the kids much and she was so lonely for them. My mother's heart was about to break into a million pieces, but I knew she was where she needed to be. If only we could have visited her every day, that would have made it much more bearable.

November 20, 2020: She was taken for an abdominal and chest scan. This was on a Friday. As I mentioned earlier, we learned that not much is done on the weekends at a hospital. We were informed the following day that lab results would not be ready until the following Monday or Tuesday, but the National Jewish Hospital in Denver was consulting with the providers at St. Luke's Presbyterian Hospital about her condition. Multiple vials of blood were drawn, and again, we waited, feeling frustrated and anxious as the weekend passed.

Laurie's emotions were off the charts. A combination of high fever, all the powerful drugs she was being given, and the unknown were very stressful on her mind and body. She befriended a nurse, and they developed a friendship. She just needed someone to talk to! Laurie was a people person. She was on high doses of steroids, and this caused her to have insomnia despite the drugs to counter it. Her blood pressure was erratic, and her pulse would go up and down. I kept the phone busy calling prayer warriors when they weren't texting me for updates.

Ian got a call from one of her doctors and was informed that they suspected Laurie did not have cancer at all. This was an unexpected but wonderful bit of news to hear. I immediately thought of the trauma the Carlsbad doctors put our family through. How could they have made such a terrible mistake? This was the reason God did not open the doors for M.D. Anderson.

November 22, 2020: I awoke to a distressing text from Laurie, "Mom, I don't know if I'm going to make it out of here." She was mentally and emotionally spent. She hadn't been able to sleep in weeks and I was very worried about her. My hotel room was directly across the hall from Ian, and I wondered silently if he was also getting distressing texts. He told me later that yes, she was asking him to get her out of there. We were as upset as anyone could imagine. I spent many alone hours in my hotel room with Jesus. There were hours that I had no words and just sat in His presence. There were times that I cried out to Him in desperation for my daughter. I told Him one time that I was relating to Mary when she had to see her son crucified and suffering. How did she endure watching Jesus die on a cross? My spirit felt a strong connection to how she must have hurt. I told God that as a mother, I was petitioning Him for my daughter to be healed. I know a mother's prayers are important to Him. I wrote my prayers down. I sang praise songs and worshiped Him and there were days that I didn't ask for anything except for Him to just sit beside me and put His arms around me. I praised Him constantly and He spoke many, many times to me. He filled me with peace for another day and that's what it was for the entire time. . . one day at a time. . . sometimes one hour at a time. His grace was and is sufficient. He taught me so much during this journey and I will forever be changed. The main lesson was about surrender—something I had a very difficult time with.

Chapter 9 GOD, PLEASE SEND US SOMEONE SMART

Ian and I desperately wanted to help Laurie. We decided if we could not go to her room that we could at least let her see us. She was on the eighth floor in room 813 at St. Luke's Presbyterian Hospital. It was connected to the Colorado Blood Cancer Institute where she went on the first day to be admitted. She was feeling a little better now and was able to walk for the physical therapist. Her mood was a little more positive now that she thought she was cancer free. We texted back and forth and asked her to tell us what she saw as she looked out her window. She texted us pictures of the landscape from her view. Ian and I drove around until we figured out which window was hers. After we discovered her room, she turned on the flashlight on her phone and waved to us. We were talking to each other as she watched us waving to her on the sidewalk below her window. It was amazing how that lifted our spirits. Laurie seemed to mellow after we did this, and the distressing texts diminished for the most part. Thank you, God.

Afterward, Ian and I drove around the campus once again and thanked God for His goodness as we prayed for her protection. We asked God to touch every patient in the hospital and to bless each family represented there. We felt God's peace as we drove back to the hotel.

November 23, 2020: Laurie was scheduled for another lung biopsy. Ian wrestled with giving permission to put her through another invasive surgery, but he was told that the biopsy in Carlsbad was not sufficient. (Not surprising.) More tissue samples were needed to do further studies. Reluctantly, he agreed to give the green light for another biopsy because we needed answers. She had improved the past 24 hours and had not required the use of oxygen. The medical team felt she was strong enough to tolerate the procedure. The great news was that they allowed Ian to be with her pre-op and post-op in the recovery room. All went well by God's mercy and the quality time they spent together was healing for both. He stayed until he was asked to leave, and it was difficult to say goodbye to her. I have pictures of her that he took, and she was beautiful even in her surgical gear. She was smiling and that was so good to see.

Later, the nurse texted me pictures of her surgery site. The entire left side of her body was bruised and traumatized. I was hurt when I saw the pictures. She had been through so much! This biopsy was much more invasive, and she had more pain and more stitches this time. Our prayer was for definite answers now. She was so brave and strong, and her endurance and resilience amazed us all, including the medical team. She was always a fighter, and she will always be my brave hero.

In my hotel room, I found myself humming some songs that God put on my heart. Laurie and I had a private joke about how we always hum. It's something we do and sometimes are not even aware of, but we would often tease each other about it. Reid has the humming gene also. I felt like I should only praise God on this day. I sang "Hallelujah," and thanked Him for His goodness. I praised Him through the mystery illness and reminded myself that He is with us through the good times and through the bad times. He never left us. I rebuked fear and declared that our family would not partner with the enemy and his lies. When we praise God, He shows up. He waits for us and longs for our communion with Him. His presence is so sweet and the atmosphere completely changes. There is absolutely nothing like His presence.

November 26, 2020: Thanksgiving Day was honestly the worst Thanksgiving I've ever experienced in some ways, but it was also a demonstration of God's goodness. Ian and I were at the Marriott and because of COVID, our only option for dining was to order take-out. We had planned to spend our Thanksgiving eating take-out in our hotel room, but to our surprise and thanks to some amazing friends, we were treated to a wonderful delivery of food! My Abilene friend, Donna, has a son, John, who lives in the Denver area. He knocked on our door with a huge box from Boston Market with enough food to feed us for several days. We had turkey and dressing with all the sides included. How thoughtful of John to take time off from his Thanksgiving to make our day so special. He may never realize how much that meant to us and how much we appreciated him. Yes, there are still good people on this planet!

Unfortunately, Laurie started to decline again, to our disappointment. She had another bone marrow biopsy performed. She was experiencing shortness of breath and her oxygen saturation was lower than the normal range. She had been off oxygen up until this point but required six liters now. The sores in her mouth and throat were causing severe discomfort and she was unable to eat or swallow without pain. Her heart rate was racing as high as 120 beats per minute and her blood pressure was low. She was sent for a CT scan of her throat and due to high doses of steroid being administered, she required insulin to bring down high blood sugars. She was not a diabetic, but steroids have this side effect. The doctor called Ian and told him they were considering transferring Laurie to Critical Care so she could be monitored more closely. Fortunately, she began to gradually improve thanks to the power of many prayers from family and friends.

November 27, 2020: The biopsy report from her bone marrow revealed that there was no infection. We also got the long-awaited news that confirmed Laurie did not have cancer anywhere in her body! The diagnosis we received in Carlsbad of end-stage cancer was a cruel misdiagnosis. Many times, I wanted to call them, but I never did. I pray that no other family will have to go through this because it was devastating. I am so very thankful that we are a family of faith and that we didn't take their word for it. Always, always get a second opinion, or a third. . . I thank God that He opened the door to Denver and that we didn't send her back to Roswell to give up like we were told to do!

So, now, we were still without a diagnosis. We knew what she didn't have, but the rest remained a mystery. The lung biopsy was sent to a premier respiratory facility at the National Jewish Hospital for a second opinion. Again, we played the waiting game and with this being Thanksgiving weekend, it would be delayed even longer.

She was treated for abnormal blood work. Her hemoglobin was very low, and she required two units of packed cells, leaving the doctors baffled as to why her iron was low. Her magnesium level was also low, so she was treated for that with supplements. She was started back on high doses of steroids and continued to require the bad tasting mouthwash for the persistent thrush that refused to go away. She was sent for more CT scans and X-Rays. I couldn't help but be concerned about all the radiation she was being exposed to and all the highly addictive drugs for pain she was getting round the clock. I know that should have been the least of my worries, but we would deal with that later I told myself.

November 29, 2020: Laurie's condition started to improve after all the treatments and high doses of steroids she received. The steroids were keeping her alive. Long-term steroid use can cause brutal side effects such as increased risk of infections, osteoporosis, diabetes, high blood pressure, insomnia, excessive bruising, and swelling to name a few. Knowing this, we still felt this was our only choice because it was helping her so much. With all the outward evidence of side-effects, she still looked beautiful to us. She always tried to give us a smile and one of us could always make her laugh a little.

The T-Cell clonality test that we had waited weeks for finally came back confirming she had no cancer. This was also verified by the National Jewish Hospital and brought us great comfort. These tests were very extensive and went down to the molecular level of her DNA. We were totally at rest knowing she had no cancer, but not at peace about what exactly she did have. This mystery disease had everyone baffled.

She was not requiring oxygen now and her oxygen saturations were staying up consistently. She reported feeling much better and was beginning to get back to her feisty self. She began eating better and told us the highlight of her day was filling out her menu for the next meal. She had not eaten in so long, everything tasted good to her. She texted us pictures of her food trays and it was quite entertaining and funny. She felt well enough to order Christmas gifts online while lying in her bed. We were all very encouraged. I have saved all the many texts she sent me through the years, and I cherish every single word, although they are difficult to read sometimes.

Chapter 10 HAPPINESS IS DENVER, COLORADO IN OUR REAR VIEW MIRROR

At last—we finally heard music in our ears when they called Ian to tell us Laurie would be discharged to go home. They believed because she had improved so much that she would continue to heal at home with high doses of steroids and being closely monitored by labs and scans. She would see a new Pulmonologist in Albuquerque as soon as possible for follow-ups. Although her lungs were still not totally free of nodules, the last scans had revealed much improvement and showed much diminishment. She was also instructed to see her PCP as soon as she got home for follow-up care.

December 9, 2020: What a glorious day! When we picked her up at the hospital, I was expecting to see her waiting in a wheelchair like most patients being discharged. But no, not Laurie. She was with her nurse standing next to the curb with her hand on her hip anxiously waiting for us to get her out of that place! I will always remember the big grin on her face. She was so happy and excited to see us. After loading the van with all her belongings, we were on a mission to get on the highway and get out of town as soon as possible. As happy as we were to see Denver to get her admitted into a hospital, we were even more excited to get her out of town!

Our trip home was uneventful with no oxygen tanks required. We stopped to eat and take bathroom breaks, and before we knew it, we were turning into their residential neighborhood in Roswell, NM. I took a picture of the beautiful New Mexico sunset that evening. It was the most beautiful canvas that God created, splashed with brilliant corals, pinks, purples, crimsons, and almost a neon orange color as it graced the sky. It was as if God was saying, "Welcome home, Laurie. . . I painted this just for you!" His presence was tangible.

As we turned into the garage, Erynn, Reid, and Carol greeted us with huge smiles and laughter. Carol had prepared a delicious meal of roast beef and it tasted good after our long drive home and weeks of fast food. Erynn and Reid had surprised everyone with a display of Christmas decorations, and they had put up the tree. Our happiness oozed out of us as we celebrated Laurie's homecoming and God's goodness.

The following days, Laurie was better but still had a long way to go to regain her strength and muscle tone. She had been in bed so long and she would need consistent physical therapy. She had lost so much weight, that I was afraid her little legs would snap with the slightest pressure. The steroids had kept her alive, but the side effects were evident with puffiness and lack of sleep. She was positive though and so elated to be home, she was determined to rebound as quickly as possible. The first thing on her agenda was to get their Christmas cards mailed. I don't think any of us could have been any happier than we were that day, including her co-dependent dogs who would not let her get an inch away from them.

Still with no true diagnosis, we were told that she definitely had an auto-immune disease of unknown origin and angiitis of the central nervous system. We were given hope that she would continue to improve, and the doctors would continue to study her slides and tissue samples looking for much needed answers. The doctors said they would be in communication with her PCP and Pulmonologist in Albuquerque. We believed God would still send us someone smart who could figure all this out. Oftentimes we felt this was just one big guessing game that no one could seem to agree on.

I stayed until I was confident that she was going to be okay, and I knew that Ian, Erynn, and Reid would be more than attentive to her. Ian had decided to resign from the law firm and dedicate his time to his family that needed him. I will always love and admire this man that God sent to Laurie. He is rare indeed and totally devoted to his wife and children. I've watched him care for Laurie and my heart is full.

It was difficult to leave Roswell. I just wanted to stay and hold her hand...but my sister, Katy, had been holding down the fort for me all the time I had to be away, and she needed to take care of her family. I will forever be grateful to her for being there for me.

December 13, 2020: I left for Abilene, TX. We had made plans for me to return on Christmas Eve and stay awhile. I still had shopping to do for my grandchildren. I had not bought one thing because our life had been put on hold for months. After rivers of happy tears flowed, I spent the rest of my trip praising God from whom all blessings flow. I sang, I prayed, and I praised Him as He gave us all another beautiful sunset. Life was good. God is good.

Chapter 11 CHRISTMAS BLESSINGS

God is merciful. He gave the family such a beautiful Christmas together. They were getting last minute shopping done and making Laurie rest as much as possible. At times, she was determined to do more than she should have but she learned to pace herself after realizing how weak she still was.

I was back in Abilene trying to readjust to my routine. I had been away so long I felt a little lost. Laurie and I texted or talked on the phone frequently throughout the days leading up to Christmas. She had begun to walk on her treadmill and was working up to more time every day. She texted me a picture of raspberry scones she had just made, so I felt confident she was getting stronger. She was making me laugh on the phone again and I was anxious to go on December 24 to spend Christmas with them.

My cousin, Sonny and his wife, Belinda (we call her Ben), and their grown son, Cale came to see me, and we had a nice visit. Our family likes to hug each other and as they were leaving, we all hugged to say our good-byes.

They called me two days later to tell me that they both tested positive for COVID although they were both asymptomatic. I was sorry for them and then I suddenly realized that I couldn't be around Laurie. I would not be able to spend Christmas in Roswell. I was also afraid to be around the rest of my family, so I stayed home until I knew I was not sick. I spent Christmas alone, but I was looking forward to going as soon as possible. I would never have risked infecting anyone, especially Laurie with her lung condition. The last thing Laurie needed was COVID!

Laurie and Ian were being extremely careful at home by not allowing visitors. Everyone was understanding and would leave meals on their picnic table. They would take turns and send out a schedule of who was cooking and what the meal would be. I will forever be grateful to their Roswell friends for all the kindness they showed our family. The body of Christ is incredible in the way that they show love toward others.

Laurie's forty-fifth birthday was on January 18th. I had planned to come the day before so we could celebrate together. We texted pictures back and forth and talked on FaceTime as they were opening their Christmas gifts. I had the impression that I should go sooner than the 17th. I told Laurie and Ian that I felt I should come a week earlier on January 9th instead. I don't know why I changed my mind because I was scheduled to work on the week of the ninth and I had to cancel all those days. I felt an urgency to go early, and besides, I just missed her.

January 9, 2021: This was a Thursday. We had such a fun visit, but the days went by much too quickly. Laurie felt fairly well but mentioned that she was glad I didn't come on Christmas day because she felt really bad. She had a few times during my visit that she wanted to go lie down, but we just thought it was because her body had been through so much trauma, and she would need to rest often. She wasn't having trouble breathing anymore and everything seemed like it was returning to normal. Her appetite was fairly good, and she was still exercising on her treadmill and busy most days talking to friends on the phone. She assured me for the most part, she was doing much better. She did tell me that she had been having headaches and trouble sleeping and I suggested she see her PCP about that. She agreed and I was happy that she was going to make an appointment the following week. I encouraged her to rest more and not worry about cooking and cleaning because Ian, Erynn, and Reid were more than happy to pitch in.

I observed that her frail body was still badly bruised. Her back, side, and abdomen were purple. She had been receiving Lovenox, a blood thinner, in the hospital to prevent blood clots and that caused bruising across her abdomen. Her skinny little arms were dotted with needle marks from blood draws and IV's, and she was experiencing pain under her ribs where the last lung biopsy had been performed. She was unable to wear a bra and was miserable. I bought her sports bras, but she couldn't stand anything to touch that area. The active wear that I brought her was too large because she had lost so much weight and I told her I would return them for a smaller size. My poor baby girl. How I wish I could have taken the pain and trauma from her.

I didn't want to leave her, but she kept trying to convince me she was doing much better. If I hadn't seen all the bruises, I might have been more convinced. She promised me she would see the doctor about the headaches, and I was relieved that Ian was taking such good care of her.

When I left, I told her I would exchange her birthday clothes and put some more surprises in the box for her birthday. I told her that she had to wait until her birthday to open it though. I will always regret telling her that. She never got to open her gift from me. Little did I know that when I left that Sunday, that would be the last time I ever felt her arms hugging me goodbye. That would be the last time she would tell me that she loved me and the last time we would communicate verbally in person.

Chapter 12 AIRLIFTED TO THE UNKNOWN

When traveling, our family always texts or calls when we are home safely. I reported I was home, and she replied, telling me how much she enjoyed our visit and thanking me again for the gifts.

January 13, 2021: I sent her several texts on Monday morning but heard no response, so I was hoping she was with her doctor to talk about the headaches. I texted her again later Monday evening and only got a short response that was not like her at all. It said, "Been busy... have headache." I was beginning to get worried, so I texted Ian to check on her. It wasn't long before Ian texted me and said, "Just FYI, if you haven't heard from Laurie much, she hasn't felt great the last few days." He proceeded to tell me he called her doctors, and they ran some lab tests just to make sure there was no infection anywhere. Those tests were clear. They had a Zoom call scheduled for later that evening with the Pulmonologist and they had planned to do an MRI later just to be safe. I had a feeling something was not right, and he told me that she had become very confused. The Pulmonologist said to skip the MRI and take her to the ER in Roswell as soon as possible. They were doing labs right then and the Pulmonologist gave her sedation for the MRI.

He texted me later and said she was back in the exam room, they were waiting for the report, and she was sedated and asleep. The nurse mentioned to Ian it might be fungal, but that was just her opinion.

I asked Ian while we were waiting what he meant when he said she became confused? He said that one of her friends had planned to bring pizza over and they could talk through the patio window, being careful not to come in contact with her. He said that totally confused her. She was stressing about what kind of pizza to order and was stressing if everyone would like what was ordered and it was just totally uncharacteristic of her to be acting like this. She had also told Erynn while in the kitchen that she had to fix a sandwich for YaYa (my name). Erynn said, "Mom, YaYa is not here, she's in Abilene." Laurie then said, "Of course, what am I thinking?" Her confusion progressively got worse throughout the day. He promised to call me as soon as he knew anything. I asked him if she knew who he was and he replied sadly, "No."

It wasn't long until he called me back with news that rocked our world. Laurie's MRI was abnormal. Her brain had nodules like the ones in her lungs. She was very, very sick and was being airlifted to UNMH - the University of New Mexico Hospital in Albuquerque. He and the kids were throwing some clothes in the car and driving to Albuquerque, and he promised to keep me updated when he got news.

January 14, 2021: She was still in the ER at UNMH and waiting to be transferred to a room as soon as one became available. COVID was rampant and the hospital was full of patients. Nurses were overworked and things weren't very organized. Ian was not allowed to be with Laurie. God help us.

Ian spent countless hours getting files and history for the providers. Laurie's doctors were in communication with the team in Albuquerque and she was finally admitted to the ICU Neurology floor. Ian said they were preparing her for a lumbar spinal tap, and she was sedated. She didn't appear to have meningitis, but they were checking for everything. She had infectious disease and neurology checking as well as pathologists and multiple others attending to her. Another PET scan was done. An EEG and EKG were done, and she was put on a prophylactic anti-seizure medication. As a nurse, I knew this was bad, but I asked Ian just how bad is it? He said she went from talking on the phone with friends and walking on the treadmill on Monday, functional but more confused Tuesday, to pretty much out of it by Wednesday morning. When he asked her if she knew who he was, she replied, "No." I had no words. Ian was devastated and my heart was breaking.

What could I do? We weren't allowed in the hospital. COVID restrictions were very strict, and they wouldn't even allow Ian in. It was the most helpless feeling in the world. Should I stay in Abilene? I couldn't afford to pay for a hotel indefinitely, and no one knew how long she would be there. I told Ian I would stay home until we knew more and then I would come as soon as possible. It was so hard not to be there.

At first, she was consistently able to tell the doctors her name when they asked. They had started IV steroids and other IV meds. She was sleeping a lot, but hopefully soon we could FaceTime with her. She had to have a nasogastric tube (NG tube) inserted through her nose to her stomach for nourishment and for medications. This procedure is very unpleasant, and I was traumatized knowing how traumatized she must be, especially all alone and surrounded by total strangers.

January 16, 2021: She started declining and didn't know her name today, but when they said her name, she would respond by opening her eyes.

They continued to do more scans and every test imaginable. Ian was still not allowed to be with her and the communication at this hospital was very poor. He was calling often for updates and not always getting answers.

Poor Ian—between trying to get communication from the medical team and me texting him all the time and him trying to hold it together for Erynn and Reid, I don't know how he would have made it without his strong faith. We were all a mess. I prayed for a miracle and someone smart. I prayed until I couldn't pray anymore.

There was constant activity in her room. Tests, more tests, and procedures followed—scans, MRIs, CT scans, sonograms, PET scans, multiple X-Rays, and dozens of vials of blood drawn. She had been stuck so many times a central line had to be inserted. With much sadness and prayer Ian finally agreed to give permission for a brain biopsy. They were doing genome testing at the molecular level at the University of California in San Francisco, and high dose steroid therapy was being administered. Doctors at the NIH (National Institute of Health in Washington) were consulted. The senior clinician of Lymphomatous Malignancies Branch, experts in lymphoproliferative disorders, and the Neuropathologists at NIH and Cleveland Clinic reviewed the lung and brain biopsies and slides.

There were more spinal fluid biopsies, and a procedure called plasmapheresis was started. She had the NG tube removed and had a feeding tube surgically inserted in her stomach. This was hard for me to grasp. It seemed so final. I was finally able to calm down after Ian talked to me and told me that this would help save her life with the necessary nourishment she needed. If I could have died right THEN, I would have. It was almost more than I could bear, imagining her poor body and all she was going through all alone.

We couldn't give up!!! She still had a long life ahead of her. She had graduations and weddings to attend and help plan. She had future grand babies to spoil and a mother who couldn't live without her. She had a husband that adored her and two amazing children who needed their mother. She had three brothers and their families that she prayed for and loved deeply. She loved her family and friends, and we all needed her here with us.

The only conclusion the entire medical team agreed on was that she had an unidentified auto-immune disease and angiitis of the central nervous system. All the best doctors and pathologists from M.D. Anderson, Johns Hopkins, NIH, the Cleveland Clinic, and Baylor hospital were consulting. They had never seen a case like this and were all baffled. She was their mystery case. I asked one of her many doctors one day if he had ever had a case like this. He shook his head and replied, "No, never in my 30 years of practice." I just wanted to run up and down the hall and scream or throw something or bite someone. I'm just being honest. At times, this was just unbearable. With the no visitors rule, I was tormented thinking about my sweet girl lying there all alone being poked, prodded, and unable to verbalize.

The nursing shortage was evident at this hospital. They often had traveling nurses which resulted in different people every day. Nothing was consistent. No one wanted to work, and the CNAs were overworked. We learned quickly to question everything that was done and document every word. Ian was the master note taker, and I was so thankful for him.

Chapter 13 THE SWIRLING ATMOSPHERE OF UNCERTAINTY

I am not a person who likes confrontations or drama of any kind, but on a few occasions, I got upset with some of the people who were responsible for Laurie's care. She was unable to FaceTime at this point and our only source of information was when we were able to talk to the caregivers. We clung to every word and looked forward to our communication with the staff every day. Any news was better than not knowing what was going on.

Some days we had great nurses. Other days we were treated as if we were bothering them, and that was hard. We understood they were understaffed and stressed. We respected that and always complimented them and thanked them. We bought several meals at various times for the staff to show our appreciation. We went out of our way to show our appreciation and gratitude for the care they were giving to Laurie. We had a few nurses that told us they were praying for her. One nurse said God would wake her up during the night to pray. That touched us and I will always wonder what their prayers accomplished in the spirit or perhaps prevented.

Several times, Ian and I discussed transferring Laurie to another medical center but each time we were faced with COVID and if anyone would even have a room for her. Also, she was so very ill, and we honestly didn't know if she would survive the transport. We also did not want her to endure anymore invasive testing or treatments, knowing a new hospital would want to do their own tests. There were so many factors involved. We had people suggesting we do this, and we do that, all meaning well. Ian had multiple people texting and calling him with questions and suggestions about specific conditions or whether tests for specific conditions had been performed. Everyone meant well and were just trying to help. Each time, either in Denver or in Albuquerque, he would ask the providers and each time they would confirm that those had been considered and tested for—sometimes more than once. It was difficult to know what to do. We wanted the very best for her and did all we knew to do. She was totally nonverbal now and unable to voice her feelings. Our security was in Jesus and our trust in Him. He was the only one that brought us comfort when the darkness closed in on us. We had to silence the outside voices and focus on our quiet time with the Lord.

January 18, 2021: Today was Laurie's 46th birthday. At last, the nurse was able to put the phone in front of Laurie so we could FaceTime with her. Although she was nonverbal, she could hear us and see us. Erynn and Reid were happy to see their mom, although it was hard for them to see her so sick. She would make expressions with her face, and we felt like she was aware of some of the times we talked to her even though she had trauma to her brain. We reminded her it was her birthday.

Due to COVID, the patients were required to share rooms. Ian and I were not happy about that. Because of her brain trauma she was extremely sensitive to noise and chaos. There was always noise in the background when we would FaceTime, and we could sense the stress it was causing her. Finally, after a lot of prayer and intervention by Ian's aunt who had some influence, we were able to get her into a private room and that was much more peaceful for her (and us)! God answered our prayer for her to have peace.

At last, the hospital lifted the "no visitor" rule. Ian was allowed to be with her from 11:00 am to 7:00 pm. I started sleeping much better knowing he would be there taking care of her. I was later approved to visit her and drove to Albuquerque as often as possible. It was an eight-hour drive from Abilene, but I would have driven twice that just to see her and hold her hand. On my first trip, my long-time friend, Jana accompanied me. I didn't want to drive in Albuquerque alone and I will always be grateful for her company and prayers. After that, I felt comfortable by myself.

I wasn't prepared when I first saw my girl. She had an incision with 12 stitches on the upper right side of her temple and scalp area where the brain biopsy was performed. Of course, part of her head was shaved, and her hair was matted with glue from the multiple EEGs. It was hard to see her like this, but I was so grateful to finally be with her—she looked beautiful to me. I was amazed at her strength and courage. I was, and still am, so incredibly proud of her. It was God's mercy that she never appeared to be in pain after we got to start visiting her—at least I never observed it.

She had lost her swallow reflex due to the nodules that caused inflammation and swelling on her brain stem. That is why she had the feeding tube surgically inserted into her stomach. She did start to feel better after she started getting nourishment this way. She had not eaten in months and had lost so much weight. My heart broke when I rubbed her body with lotion. I anointed her all over with oil and prayed over her while I was massaging her—she was anointed head to toe. I gave her pedicures because she always had her nails and toenails painted. Ian did range of motion exercises with her daily and made sure she was turned every two hours. The nursing staff was amazed that Laurie's skin integrity looked so good. They commented she looked amazing for someone who had been bedbound for so long. She had no bed sores and tried very hard to cooperate with the physical therapists, although it was very painful for her.

Ian brushed her hair every day and eventually got the EEG glue out and was gentle and patient with her. He carried on a one-man conversation with her and regularly updated about the kids' schoolwork and what was going on. He played her CD player with scriptures when he would leave for the night. He taped scriptures on her wall, and we had a framed photo of their family by her bedside. He prayed over her and blessed her. He was there every day except Wednesday mornings and when I was there. On Wednesdays he drove Erynn and Reid to Roswell and back to Albuquerque so they could continue their piano lessons. Then he would go back to the hospital and feed Laurie her dinner. He was trying to keep their life as normal as possible considering the circumstances. I love this man.

Each week we were promised pathology and lab reports. The week would pass, and the lack of news would disappoint us. You would think by now we would be used to it, but we constantly felt frustrated and disappointed. Then when we would finally get reports, they would be unidentified or inconclusive. I told Ian we must have prayed for patience sometime in our lives because God was sure teaching us about it.

Her condition was very baffling and inconsistent. On some days she responded to us by saying a few words. On other days she was unable to speak. It was an emotional roller coaster, but we celebrated each small victory. We never left her room without praying for protection over her and claiming Psalm 91—for God to strategically place guardian angels around her. We were so very grateful that she could breathe without needing oxygen. That was a huge victory that we praised God for. I did notice that when I laid my hands on her forehead and prayed, she was very still, and I believe she knew what was being said. I know her spirit knew.

Chapter 14 A LESSON OF FAITH AND TRUST

On one particular visit when I felt sure she was understanding me, I had a very difficult conversation with Laurie. I told her how proud I was of her. I told her what a great daughter she had always been and what a joy she was in my life. I told her I did not want her to leave this world, but I knew she was very tired and had endured more than most people could imagine. I gave her my blessing to quit fighting if that's what she wanted to do. I told her she had freedom in Jesus and if she wanted to go rest that would be okay with me. I assured her I would be okay and so would Ian and her children. I reminded her that she had raised two amazing kids and their faith was strong and solid. I told her that although we would miss her terribly, I knew we would see her again. I told her it was hard for me and Ian to see her suffer and my heart was breaking because she was so sick. I also told her that if she chose to keep fighting that I was her biggest cheerleader. I would be there for her as long as she needed me. We locked eyes once again and I feel confident that she understood me. I just knew. That was the hardest conversation I've ever needed to have.

The next few days passed, and she started to decline. Due to the hospital staff's poor communication, Ian was not informed that her steroids had been decreased. As I said earlier, the steroids kept her alive during these times. We were not happy about this miscommunication. Her steroids were not supposed to be decreased right now! She was transferred to the ICU, and we nearly lost her due to the hospital's incompetence. When I received the doctor's call at midnight, he told me her pupils were dilated and not responding to light. That's how close to losing her we came. After the steroids were increased, she eventually improved enough to leave ICU and go back to her room in the neurology unit. She had a whole new set of bruises after that incident. It hurt me knowing that a life-threatening episode could have been totally avoided.

We celebrated when she would say a word. We cheered when she told the nurse, "Ouch, that hurts!" as she was getting an injection of blood thinner in her abdomen. It was a huge celebration when she was able to start eating solid foods again and we didn't have to tube feed her. I made a special trip to La Madeline's restaurant to get her crème brulee and she loved it. It was a joy to feed her real food and to watch her enjoy her meal.

At my house I have two wooden plaques on my wall that I bought when Laurie got sick. One says, "Believe in Miracles," and the other says, "Celebrate Everything." Every time I see them, I'm reminded of how precious life is. Every second is a gift from our creator. A lot can happen in 24 hours. Lives can change. I tell friends and family how much they mean to me now. I have learned not to take anything for granted because it can be taken away in an instant. If someone is in our life, God put them there for a reason.

As the weeks passed and we still had no definite diagnosis of this mystery disease that had ravished Laurie's body, the nurses and doctors grew very attached to Laurie and Ian. When they spoke of Ian, they told me how much they admired him as a husband. He was attentive and took excellent care of her. They said that my daughter was well-loved. I knew this but it made me proud to hear it from others. She was treated with respect by the ones that knew her and Ian.

The team of providers had multiple meetings about the next step to take concerning the plan of treatment. She was fairly stable and able to eat now. They talked to Ian about plasmapheresis treatments. It's a process where the blood is filtered out and the plasma is separated from the red blood cells. Unhealthy plasma is swapped for healthy plasma before the blood is returned to the body. After these treatments were done, she appeared to feel better for a few days. The initial plan was to do these three times weekly for several weeks.

After administering the plasmapheresis treatments, they talked to Ian about starting a round of chemo (Cyclophosphamide) once monthly for six months. Even though she did not have cancer they told us chemo is also used for other illnesses. Honestly, they didn't know what else to do. It took several weeks for Ian and the doctors to come to a decision because of the risks, but they finally decided to go ahead. We prayed that we made the right decision. We wanted something done! We felt like so much time had been wasted waiting on test results and we needed to do something—anything!

After the first infusion, she seemed to improve a little. She was more alert and became more verbal. She continued to eat and enjoyed her food. She even hummed occasionally! We were very hopeful and encouraged.

However, four weeks later, after the second infusion, she started to decline. She became nonverbal again and quit eating. She required being fed through the tube once again and we were devastated. She had made such progress and now this setback took the wind out or our sails. I reminded God that He was still God in the valley.

Her vitals were stable, and we were praying that she would bounce back once again. I had to go back to Abilene for a few days because of my job but I promised I would be back in a few days. As I was leaving Albuquerque, I felt extremely sad about leaving. I was crying and having a heart-to-heart talk with Jesus and asking for more mercy for Laurie. As I was on I-40, I glanced up over the freeway and noticed an enclosed walkway for pedestrians. There was a man walking his dog directly over my vehicle as I drove under it. I immediately heard the word "Trust." I knew this was the voice of God. It was all too familiar to me. I asked what He wanted to teach me. I talked to Him and said "Yes, I understand trust. Are you showing me that this man trusts the designer of this bridge to protect him from oncoming traffic below him? Are you showing me that he trusts this to shelter him and his dog from danger?" There was silence. Next, I heard God say to me, "Julie, do you trust me—the architect and designer of your daughter? Do you trust me with Laurie? Do you trust me with Laurie's life?"

Tears wouldn't stop as I told Him, "Yes, I trust you God, I trust you with my daughter's life, may your will be done and your will alone." I knew I had been praying for my will because I didn't want Laurie to die. I learned right at that moment to totally surrender her to Jesus. There is a difference between singing the song, "I Surrender All" and actually surrendering it all. I needed to surrender the spirit of control I had. I had been trying to fix everything by praying and manipulating prayers according to my will. This was much bigger than me. I had such a spirit of heaviness that I could no longer carry it. It was weighing me down and dragging me with it. That was a special time with Jesus that I will never forget. It changed me. I did learn from it, although I can't say it was an easy lesson. I cried most of the eight hours home, but that night I slept like a baby, which was very rare. All it took was an encounter with the Holy Spirit and one simple word. . . TRUST.

Chapter 15 GRIEF BRINGS UNEXPECTED EMOTIONS

The providers called a meeting and asked Ian to be present. He was basically told they didn't know what else to do for Laurie and they were baffled because a diagnosis had not been made. They had exhausted every plan of treatment. After all those months of praying for God to send us someone smart, we still had no one. They proceeded to tell Ian that eventually the family would be faced with decisions for her long-term care. Our options were limited because she had been at UNMH since January 2021, and this was May 2021...she couldn't stay at the hospital forever. They suggested she go to rehab and then after that she would need to go to a skilled nursing facility because they felt she required medical care that could not be provided at home.

With a heavy heart, Ian called me and gave me the update. I wish I could say that I remained calm but all I could hear was "nursing home." No! I will not put my daughter in a nursing home. I'm a nurse and I've seen too many skilled nursing facilities and how they operate—even the best ones are unacceptable, in my opinion. Ian was also having a difficult time processing this information and I wasn't helping with my reaction. My mind started swirling with options. I could move to Roswell and take care of Laurie. I could feed her through the tube, and I could see that she had the best of care. I would do whatever was necessary. I told God if He would heal Laurie, then we wouldn't have this problem to deal with. (I'm sure God needed me to tell Him that).

After a good cry and much prayer, I calmed down. I apologized to Ian, and he graciously received it. I heard that word again—"Trust." I had to make the decision to give this to God. I was not in control, and I could not fix things. I prayed God's will over Laurie's life and was reminded of this scripture: "I will sing of your strength, in the morning I will sing of your love; for you are my fortress, my refuge in times of trouble." (Psalm 59:16)

Because of the inflammation on Laurie's brain stem, she was physically limited. She required repositioning every two hours and was unable to communicate with us, making it very hard to know if she was comfortable. This was a day that I would release all the months of pent-up anxiety and frustrations. As I walked into her room at the beginning of visiting hours, I saw her in a sitting position on the bed totally slumped over to the left side. She was actually touching the bed rail with her head. Her head and neck had no support and of course she was unable to push the call button. My heart broke into a million pieces. I had no idea how long she had been left unattended, but five minutes would have been too long. She looked extremely uncomfortable and helpless lying there. I had my phone in my hand, so I quickly took a photo, then rearranged her with pillows to provide proper alignment and support. I massaged her neck and told her repeatedly how sorry I was.

There is an older movie that was popular in 1983 titled, Terms of Endearment starring Shirley McLain and Debra Winger. In one particular scene in the hospital the daughter (Debra Winger) was dying with cancer and needed pain medication. It was past time for her medication because the nurse was late. The mother (Shirley McLain) lost her dignity as she walked to the nurses' station and shouted for them to give her daughter pain medication! She just wanted her daughter taken care of and didn't want her to hurt. On this day, I was Shirley McLain. I went to the nurses' station, only to see a group standing around eating and laughing. I held the picture of Laurie up and asked them to tell me if this was acceptable to them? I went a little crazy and it was so quiet you could have heard a pin drop. I'm not proud that I lost my temper, and I don't usually act like that, but I'm sure if it happened again, I would react the same way. I went to the Social Worker and to the Primary Attending Physician and voiced my concern and disappointment to them. The Social Worker talked to the staff and made large posters above her bed that read, "Make sure the patient has proper support for the head and neck." We are our loved ones' only advocate when they are helpless. We learned to question every procedure and every time a medication was given. So many mistakes are made in hospitals, either by error, fatigue, carelessness, or incompetency. Nurses and doctors are tired. They make mistakes because they are human. There are many excellent doctors and nurses but there are some that are unacceptable, and we had to monitor everything. Unfortunately, we weren't allowed to stay after 7:00 pm and we had to trust God to be in her room. Once again, I had to stop and remind myself that my foundation was built on Jesus and the power of His resurrection and not on my feelings. Later, I received many apologies, and I was quick to forgive. I just wanted my daughter to be treated with dignity and respect.

Things improved and the staff was much more attentive to her needs. The Social Worker communicated with me often and was very professional and caring. She gave Laurie a handmade quilt with bright colors to stimulate her brain. I appreciate all the small things she did.

Ian called me a few days later and asked me if I left a framed picture of Jesus in Laurie's room. He said it had gold writing at the bottom of the picture in Spanish. I said, "It wasn't me—who left it?"

He said it was strange because he had asked everyone, and no one knew where it came from. He said to me, "Do you want to know what it says in Spanish?" Well of course I wanted to know, and he replied, "Jesus, I trust you." Wow… I hear you God. That five-letter word, that changed me!

I discovered that just when we are at our breaking point, when we feel we may just die, God shines His light in the dark places. He gives us just enough grace and mercy to go another day. I call these moments "kisses of mercy."

We had many God "kisses" through this journey that can't be denied. My dear friends, Laurie and Bob, arranged for me to receive prayer from some of the church elders at their home and that meant so much to me. I didn't realize how much I needed prayer until I felt the heaviness lift. We prayed for God's will to be done and it was a sweet time of fellowship. I left feeling energized and refreshed. That's what prayer does…The Holy Spirit comes when invited and we welcome that. It is so beautiful.

Chapter 16 THE VALLEY OF DARKNESS

May 13, 2021: I was back in Abilene for a few days and had made plans to drive to Albuquerque on May 19th. I felt a nudge, almost an urgency to make plans to go earlier. I texted Ian and asked if Sunday the 17th would be ok for them. Yes, they would be fine with that and were looking forward to seeing me. I was anxious to see them as well.

May 18, 2021: After arriving the night before, I was awake early and anticipating the day with Laurie. Visiting hours started at 11:00 am, so I was drinking coffee and enjoying the quiet time. My phone rang and it was Ian. I will forever remember this call as I felt life was being sucked out of me.

Somewhere deep inside my being I felt as if I was in a vortex of dread and swirling darkness. With a heaviness in Ian's voice, he told me that Laurie had been rushed to the ICU early that morning. . . she had a major brain bleed. I don't think either of us knew what else to say but we agreed to meet in front of the hospital as soon as he could get there. I don't remember driving across the street or parking in the parking garage. I felt as if I was walking underwater in slow motion and unable to walk against the current. As I stood numb outside waiting for Ian, I noticed people coming and going and laughing as they talked on their phones, most in conversations with others as if it was just another day. I wanted to scream and ask them if they didn't know this was a very bad day? Didn't they know my daughter was in ICU with blood collecting in her brain? How could they be laughing and talking as if nothing was wrong? What's wrong with these people? This was insanity.

We were there before visiting hours started but the doctor told Ian we were to come up to ICU as soon as we could get there. After being hassled at the door for what seemed like forever, we were finally given a pass. I was almost prepared to be Shirley McLain again but thank goodness I didn't go there. I don't think I had the fight in me at this point.

We were led into the Neurology ICU by a nurse who showed us to Laurie's room. We were not prepared for this. Our beautiful girl was hooked up to so many different tubes and monitors, it was ridiculous. Her face and eyelids were swollen, and she had fresh bruises noticeable on her arms and across her chest. She looked so totally helpless and was heavily sedated, unable to open her eyes, or move her body. I grabbed her hand and unlike all other times in the past, she did not grip my fingers. She felt lifeless. I made sure I could feel her pulse and it was there. Our hearts were broken in a million different pieces. I could not find words to pray, and I just said, "Jesus, Jesus, Jesus" over and over again. He was there and He understood our grief.

Shortly, the team of doctors came in and explained how serious her condition was. They explained about the stroke and showed us the image of her CT scan revealing a large area on the top frontal lobe on the left side of her brain that was filled with blood. They explained that the nodules on her brain stem ruptured causing a significant amount of bleeding. Surgery was not an option due to the inflammation in her brain and they warned us that she could simply stop breathing at any time. They told us she had five to seven days at the most. We had heard this before. My nurse's voice told me that my daughter will soon meet Jesus, but my mother's voice told me it's not over and she will pull through this—she's a fighter.

After the medical team left us alone with Laurie, I can't describe the agony we felt. It was incredibly hard to see this vibrant, funny, and full of life adult child of mine like this. Will she ever hum again? Will she ever squeeze my hand again? Will we ever see her pretty blue eyes again? God—this world is a hard place to be. Take me and give life to Laurie.

We agreed to transfer her to a private suite large enough for Ian and I to stay with her 24/7. She was going to be on comfort care, and they promised they would make sure she did not have pain.

Ian and I made phone calls to the family and to our chain of prayer warriors. Between calls we cried like babies, and we never left sweet Laurie's side except to take turns to go shower and change clothes. We had some sweet nurses and felt that she was being treated with dignity and respect.

Although she was unable to respond verbally or physically, I will always believe she could hear us. Toward the end, she suddenly turned her head toward Ian and opened her right eye a tiny bit and tried to say something to him but was unable to speak. I've often wondered what she wanted to say. Maybe she saw a host of angels—maybe she just wanted to say "goodbye" or say "I love you" …we will never know, but that's why I believe she could hear us. She tried really hard, because prior to that she had been unable to turn her head. She didn't start getting pain medications until later when her breathing began to get labored.

Laurie has always been a private person like me. Our family respects that, so in her honor I will not describe her last few days on this earth. I believe she had peace and I believe she was in the presence of Jesus. As horrible as it was for Ian and me to watch, it was a holy time also. I will always be grateful that she had God's peace. I learned so much about her strength and courage and I am so proud of her.

Chapter 17 A LEGACY OF EXCELLENCE AND GRACE

May 23, 2021: Laurie fought the good fight. How fitting that our beautiful and courageous Laurie would step out of this earthly realm into God's kingdom on Pentecost Sunday, May 23, 2021. I was with her when she took her first breath on January 18, 1975 and was with her at 5:44 am as she exhaled her last breath. My close friend and pastor, Randy Turner, said to me, "When Laurie saw the face of Jesus, He absolutely took her breath away." I believe this to be true. She loved Jesus with her whole being and we all know she is rejoicing with Him. She now has a glorified body with no more pain, disease, or tears. All fear is gone. I can't wait to join her someday soon. Until then... we continue to run this race set before us. I only pray I will do half the job my incredible daughter did. I will miss her every hour of every day. There are many reminders of her everywhere I look. Her fingerprints are everywhere. She was such a bright light.

We never got a definitive diagnosis. We've never had closure. But God was gracious to give us time to say goodbye. Death is always tragic, but I ache for those who have lost loved ones suddenly and unexpectedly. I'm thankful she was given Christmas with her family—that was such a gift. When she was airlifted to Albuquerque in January, I believe God and Laurie had a little conversation. Our family was not ready to say goodbye yet. I just wonder if God asked her if she was willing to stay here a little longer to help prepare our hearts. Knowing Laurie, I believe she said "yes" to God.

Until Laurie had the devastating brain hemorrhage, we believed she would be totally healed and restored. We never lost hope even when the medical team seemed to give up. God always gives us hope. We didn't want to see Laurie like that because she loved her life, and she was so full of life.

Nothing made her happier than being a mother and a wife. She loved her family way down deep. I never got mad at God. I cried out to Him many times in desperation and asked "Why?" I asked Him to explain things to me that I didn't understand. I asked what He would have me to learn through every trial we went through. The bottom line is that it's not about me! God's ways are not our ways. It is all about God and His glory. I believe Laurie glorified Him by her actions and her life and she has left a legacy of excellence and grace.

2 Corinthians 5:8 tells us, "We are confident, I say, and willing rather to be absent from the body, and to be present with the Lord." Hallelujah! She is no longer a prisoner in her earth suit. She is free. We praised God when her spirit left her body and Ian and I both saw her running into the arms of Jesus with a huge smile on her face. My friend Gayle had a dream of her wearing a beautiful white dress and ballet slippers. I believe God gave her that dream to bless me and give me comfort, because Laurie loved to dance. I'm painting a canvas with this vision. It was such a timely dream just when I needed it, and it has special meaning to me.

Before we left the hospital, one of the doctors stopped by to tell us how sorry she was. She cried as she said, "I don't know why, but every time I came into Laurie's room, I always got emotional." She went on to say, "That's not like me—I never do that!" I told her that we had prayed many times that Laurie's room would be anointed and perhaps she was experiencing the presence of God. She said, "Maybe you're right. . . I need to think about this."

Later, a medical student stopped by her room with an arrangement of flowers and told us how Laurie had impacted the entire medical school of 100 students. They had all been studying and researching her mystery illness. I was very honored and thanked him. As he was leaving, his eyes were moist, and I told him he would be a great doctor someday and I told him how much I appreciated his visit. I blessed him and he thanked me as he left.

That night was long and lonely, alone in my room. Even though we had time to prepare for this day it still felt surreal. I wanted to spend the next day in Albuquerque with my family, so we made plans to ride the tram to the top of Sandia Peak the next morning.

It was a beautiful sunny day overlooking the city of Albuquerque. I had bittersweet feelings about this city but was happy to be with Ian, Erynn, and Reid. We felt a strange peace on this mountain top. Part of it was relief that she was no longer a prisoner to a mystery disease that had invaded her body, and another part was because we sensed God's nearness in a tangible way. Just as Laurie had soared in the heavens, we were in a high place communicating with God. We gathered a few smooth stones from our special place, and I had the word "Trust" engraved on one for each of us. Erynn and Reid are truly amazing teenagers. Their faith is solid, and they encourage me continuously. Ian is an amazing dad and is involved in their lives with every detail. He is helping with their homeschool classes and I am surely glad that God answered my prayers and sent us "someone smart." He sent us Ian.

Chapter 18 GET THEE BEHIND ME, SATAN!

The day after our mountain top experience and fun day of being together it was time for me to go back home to Abilene. It was hard to leave. Ian, Erynn, and Reid would soon be going back to their home in Roswell after spending the last five months at Carol's house.

As I was leaving town, I stopped at a Sonic drive-in for a drink. As I was waiting for my order, I was oblivious to my surroundings and in deep thought about Laurie. Before I realized it, there was a strange man standing at my window that was rolled down. In his hand was a wad of bills. His sudden appearance startled me, and I asked what he wanted. He stared at me as he proceeded to demand that I give him change for his bills. I was getting a little uncomfortable and I told him several times that I had no change. He kept standing there and staring at me and I was in no mood to talk to anyone.

For a split second, I will be honest and tell you how I felt. I really didn't want to be on this planet without my daughter. She had been in my life for 46 years and I didn't know how I was going to live life without her. I instantly thought. . . just shoot me, mister and let's get this over with. I will instantly be with Jesus and Laurie. As suddenly as he appeared at my window, he turned around without saying another word and was gone. That was such a strange encounter.

I realized on my way home what a dark place I was in. I couldn't stay there. . . Laurie would not want that for me. That encounter convinced me that I needed to pray for deliverance, and I did just that. I had never known grief like this, and it was a scary place to be. It's normal to grieve but it's not normal to stay there. There is a season for everything.

Someone recently said to me, "It will get easier as time goes by." I disagree. I don't think it will ever get easier. I believe it will just become more familiar.

Life has forever changed but by the grace of God we will adapt and push through. His grace is sufficient. We are taught this over and over.

Life requires more trust. We must believe He is who He says He is, and He will do what He says He will do. We must believe that what He has done for others, He will do for us. This is tough, but it happens moment by moment.

God never told us to understand Him—He told us to TRUST Him. God is in the interruptions, but He's seldom in our plans. He doesn't mind if we have our plans, but He doesn't mind interrupting them either.

So, life goes on. People will continue to talk on their phones, laugh and be oblivious to other people's pain. I miss the me that used to be when Laurie was alive, and I will never truly be the same again. But we can never give up. Hopefully, because of what we experience, we will be more sensitive to others who are in pain. I pray that I have learned to be a better friend, and that I choose words wisely when speaking to those who are hurting. I pray that God will increase the spirit of intercession in me as I pray for others. I need God to navigate me through this life. Not only do I need God, but I want Him and can't imagine living life without Him. As I said earlier, it's not about me. It's not about us. It's about serving others and showing God's love. That is how Laurie lived her short life and I want to be like her when I grow up.

PRAYER FOR SALVATION - DO YOU KNOW HIM?

This book would not be complete if I didn't include this page. I'm writing this for Laurie, and she would have wanted this page more than any others. She was passionate about telling people the good news of Jesus. She loved seeing people get set free and delivered and her happiness came when one sinner repented and joined the family of God.

There is no formula for prayer. Just talk to God and pray from your heart. He knows everything about us and loves us still. Fancy words are not important to God.

So, I ask you this question: If you were to die today, do you have assurance that you would go to heaven? Be honest with yourself.

If your answer is:

I sure hope so

I think I will

I've been a good person, so I believe I'll go to heaven, then perhaps you should have a talk with Jesus about your identity and security in Him. Your answer should be a definite and positive YES. If you are saved, you will know in your heart. If you have doubts, all you need to do is confess the doubt and say a prayer for God to forgive you and save you.

It's a free gift available for everyone that believes Jesus was born of the virgin Mary, conceived by the Holy Spirit, and was crucified on the cross to be our sacrifice. He was raised three days later and now He sits at the right hand of our Father in Heaven, and He intercedes for us. "The Lord is not slow about His promise, as some count slowness, but is patient toward you, not willing for any to perish, but for all to come to repentance." (2 Peter 3:9) The Bible is alive and active. As you read the pages, ask the Holy Spirit to open your understanding and He will do that. Congratulations! You are now in the family of God. You have assurance of your eternity and now you can share your faith with others.

I want to include Laurie's obituary that Ian wrote. He honored her well.

LAURIE ELIZABETH MCKELVY

Laurie Elizabeth McKelvy passed away peacefully and immediately entered into the presence of her Lord Jesus Christ on May 23, 2021, Pentecost Sunday. She was 46 years old.

Laurie was born in Dallas, TX. on January 18, 1975, and lived her entire life in Texas until she met and married Ian D. McKelvy, whom she married on November 8, 2003 in Abilene, TX. She figured she could make something out of him, and set to work as a devoted wife. They established their family home in Roswell, NM, which quickly became her adopted hometown. They had two children together, daughter and son, Erynn and Reid.

Laurie graduated high school from Rule High School, Rule, TX, where she was a Rule Bobcat. She went on to obtain her BA. in Psychology from Texas Tech University, in Lubbock, TX. She then obtained a MS. in Counseling and Development from Texas Woman's University, in Denton, TX. But for all she learned and accomplished, like the Apostle Paul, she counted everything as loss and worthless compared to the surpassing worth of knowing Christ Jesus as her Lord and sought Him diligently. She found her calling in being a homemaker and eventually a hard-working homeschool mom, and, like everything she did, she put her heart and soul into it. She was the heart of the family home, and created an atmosphere of love, warmth, and hospitality that was palpable. She strove to make Christ the center of her home in all she did.

She spent her free time with her family but was a very loyal and thoughtful friend to many, too. She stayed very busy with her responsibilities, but found time for other things, as well. She worked for a season as secretary at her Church fellowship, Calvary Chapel of Roswell. She also volunteered as a counselor for a number of years at the Chaves County Pregnancy Resource Center. Above all else she loved the Lord and had a heart for prayer. For almost 13 years, she organized, compiled, and edited her church's weekly email prayer chain, including an original devotional thought or message that she wrote for each email. She loved and cared for her state and country and was an active citizen and voice in the political process. No doubt many of you got texts or emails from Laurie in this regard, including many elected officials. She also gave much of her time, gifts, and service, as it were, "without the right hand knowing what the left hand was doing;" but, the Lord knows.

Laurie was creative and she appreciated and was full of grace and beauty. She often made crafts and thoughtful gifts that many of you have enjoyed. And if you ever gave Laurie a gift or did anything kind for her, you undoubtedly received a very sincere, sweet, and eloquent thank you note very soon thereafter.

As gracious as she was, Laurie was also tough, and battled an illness and uncertainty over a long period of time that would have wilted the strongest man long before Laurie entered her eternal rest and reward. She showed great courage, perseverance and persistence that always marked her.

Laurie is survived by her husband, Ian, and their two children, Erynn and Reid of Roswell, NM. She is also survived by her grandmother, Eloise Newberry of Abilene, TX. and her mother, Julie Y. Boger of Abilene, TX. She was preceded in death by her father, Dr. James A. Boger. She is also survived by numerous other family whom she each loved and prayed for often by name, who know and love Laurie and who know Laurie's love, whose names do not need to be recited here; these include her beloved brothers, brothers-in-law, sisters-in-law, parents-in-law, nephews, nieces, cousins, aunts, uncles, and some not technically kin by law and brothers and sisters in Christ who were often close as kin.

A memorial service to celebrate Laurie's life will be held at Christ's Church on June 4, 2021 at 1:00 pm. Pastor Jim Suttle of Calvary Chapel Roswell will officiate.

Anderson Bethany Funeral Home is handling arrangements and online tributes.

In lieu of flowers, donations can be made in her honor to CAPE-NM, Christian Homeschool Association, the Chaves County Pregnancy Resource Center, Harvest Ministries of Roswell or Samaritan's Purse.

PHOTOS

Ian's beautiful bride.

Ian's groom's cake that I re-decorated the morning of their wedding.

Our 4-year-old ballerina

Laurie   holding   Austin,   Adam   (L),   Christopher   (back)

Christopher, Austin, and Adam

Laurie holding her co-dependent King Charles Cavaliers

Christopher and Laurie during one of our trips to Lubbock

Laurie and me on their front porch in Roswell.

Laurie soaking in the beauty and peace of Ruidoso during our Mother's Day trip.

Acknowledgements

I can't begin to thank everyone who prayed for Laurie for fear of leaving someone out. God knows who you are and so does our family and you are very dear to us. We cherish your friendship and love you very much.

Many thanks to you who sent cards and scriptures of encouragement, emailed us, sent texts, brought delicious food, sent delicious food, sent such beautiful flowers and plants and who gave the much appreciated gifts.

I want to thank the elders at Beltway Park, my home church in Abilene, Texas. Special appreciation to Randy Turner. Thanks for calling or texting regularly and for the sincere and heartfelt prayers. Our hearts were touched.

Lastly, I want to thank Jeanene Strickland and Gina Allen who spent countless hours on this project, helping this book become a reality. Thank you.